Realm of Belonging

Sapphic Poetry

by

Kieran York

Scarlet Clover Publishers, L.L.C.

Littleton, Colorado

Edited by Martha Ryan
Interior Design and Formatting by Karen D. Badger
Cover Design by Karen D. Badger
Cover Photo by Kieran York
Back Cover Photo by Brenda Starr
Cover Painting by Kieran York

Published by Scarlet Clover Publishers LLC

P.O. Box 621002
Littleton, Colorado 80162

Printed and bound in the United States of America, UK, and Europe

ISBN-13: 978-0692421772
ISBN-10: 0692421777

Realm of Belonging

by

Kieran York

Books also written by Kieran York:

Loitering on the Frontier
Touring Kelly's Poem
Night Without Time
Earthen Trinkets
Careful Flowers
Appointment with a Smile
Crystal Mountain Veils (A Royce Madison Mystery)
Timber City Masks (A Royce Madison Mystery)
Sugar With Spice (Short Fiction)
Blushing Aspen – 2014 Sappho's Corner Solo Poets Series (Poetry)

Shinney Forest Cloaks (A Royce Madison Mystery – Forthcoming)

Contributor to the Sappho's Poetry Series edited by Beth Mitchum

Wet Violets, Volume 2
Roses Read, Volume 3
Delectable Daisies, Volume 4
Fallen Petals, Volume 5

Kieran York

DEDICATION:

For Beth Mitchum, a friend of poetry, writing, publishing, and a friend of women. Thankfully, she is a friend of mine.

I'd also like to recognize all those who took the time and effort to reach for me. The women who bolstered me, and assist in making me a poet and a writer. These women are part of my Sapphic Sisterhood – and I appreciate them more than words can say.

We are all in the Realm of Belonging when we come together and work to make our literature part of the Golden Age of Sapphic Literature. I've seen so many acts of kindness within our community – and I am grateful for the assistance, the mentoring, and the acceptance of our Realm.

Beth Mitchum has been there with me every step of the way. Very simply, she knows the answers and shares them. Rogena Mitchell-Jones is my editor extraordinaire. She makes certain the words find their proper place. Karen D. Badger was there to help me rekindle the books that came before – through her diligence, they came to Scarlet Clover Publishers. She formats, designs covers, and anything it takes to make books happen. Thank you all.

All talented, brilliant women! Together women can make any dream into reality. We are women – and heck, yes, hear us roar.

Thank you, Beth!

ACKNOWLEDGEMENTS:

READERS: I'd like to acknowledge the kindness and generosity of lesfic readers. Thank you for reading lesbian fiction, and for reading my words. I appreciate your comments!

Thanks to readers, we are able to continue our heritage of offering words.

Literature belongs to us all. We develop it, groom it, and then let it stand as the historical compass of us all.

Readers – I am so proud that we together share a strong and secure Realm of Belonging.

Kieran York

Realm of Belonging

Sapphic Poetry by

Kieran York

	Page
Part One – Smiling Enchantress	1
Part Two – Soft Side	31
Part Three – Divas	57
Part Four – Sisterhood	81
Part Five – Our Path Is Time	105
Part Six – Muse of the Meadow	131
Part Seven – The Realm of Belonging	155

Part One
Smiling Enchantress

	Page
My Smiling Enchantress	2
You are Near	4
The Goddess Particle	5
Love's Asterisk	6
Dialogue with Goddesses	7
The Score Is Even	8
Wine Sidewalk	9
Unclaimed Romance	10
Savored Security	12
Trail of Perfume	13
My Flower Woman	14
Snugly	15
Almost Kindred	16
Expulsion of Love Is an Obscenity	17
Finding Her	18
Remembering Our Youth	19
Our Manifesto	20
Ripples of Flesh	22
Eloquence	23
The Vast Horizon of Age	24
Alchemist of Solitude	25
Unfolding Thought	26
Roadster	27
Where We Are	29

My Smiling Enchantress

Each night, my eyelids slowly list –
as if they are shades lowering.
And you are there –
wrapping me with protective tenderness.
When I awake to daybreak's glow my eyes focus on you –
my morning Muse.
Your frisky blue eyes open up the sky.
I witness all the world's miracles
in one Technicolor moment through your sight.
Your gentle kiss glides across my desire.
I fall into your smile.
Your voice enamors me with sonnet-induced poetry.
It is you who escorts me through each realm of romance.
You are the intriguing *happiness* book
I've memorized and cherished.
When my pages turn empty,
you issue surprise plot-twists.
I am the file you read with perfect ease
and perpetual excitement.
You recognize my lyrics and I understand your narrative.
Affection allows us to breathe precious scents
of flowers yet undiscovered.
Infatuation permits us to grasp enchantment
with a touch that becomes
our sensuous dance across forever.
You are a mystery that can't be solved,
but can eternally be pursued.
Your laughter chases away the blind spots of our day.
We tickle one another's sadness -
wherever it might be.
Adventures are teased until we locate our most affable
mirth.
With an idyllic wisp of allure -
you occupy my soul, and my heart.
We live in and through one another's benevolence.

'The Return of Destiny' might be the title
of our legacy together.
I love you with a clasp so strong
it illuminates the very corner where my hope begins.
My Muse, my woman –
you are my smiling enchantress.

You Are Near

Crouching tomorrows gather us.
Whispers that taste as if they're in love
are between our lips.
Against the architecture of your body -
my heart tolls for you.
An outline of night crowds our faces
toward sensual delicacy.
Your expressions are scribbled
in the shape of devotion.
Each poem stains my heart with your voice.
Your nearness makes my heart beat
a million songs at once.
A strand of incandescence wraps me
inside your arms.
Hours empty us into the love of one another –
one kiss chains to others.
Life scoops pleasure toward me –
you are near.

The Goddess Particle

Are we involved in being a particle of life?
Are we the Goddess particle?
We have the metabolism for reproducing.
We gather around our silence
to watch as the world whisks the skies,
and scours the globe we inhabit.
We are the silent catalyst of kindness.
Women are the Goddesses of our own miracle.
We needn't admit anyone else.
We distribute our own trust.
Each saga is a part of our mythology.
Each impulse is devoid of fiery fraudulence.
If we began idyllic quests –
where do we go in search of proof?
We have lived under the voice of misogynistic power.
Our catastrophes have shunned grave diggers
and their empty plots.
We are meant to reverberate with song.
Words are easily manufactured in our souls.
Through our lips, they pour.
We have forever cleaned and polished our thickets.
We have scrubbed our huts.
Dwellings were warmed by us.
In time's beginning, we have charred the wild beasts.
We've plucked the roots and berries.
Our breasts have fed the newborns.
Each morning we have gathered grain
and pressed the breads of life.
For all times, we have soothed, healed, and satisfied.
But when was it we agreed to be chattel?
What vote was taken to rule us?
The cudgel of strength and the vicious degree of force
have regulated us.
Still I question,
what scientist coined the word 'God' particle?
We birth all that exists.
Think that one over.

Love's Asterisk

The footnote conceded
our insouciant amendment to love.
Simmering ideas compensate for daydreams.
When we pledged love,
a calm burst of brightness happens.
Anguish was never to be regarded,
for we negotiated wisdom.
Surrender won't be launched,
and we added desire to our list of triumphs.
What cryptic sentences formed
as we perched within a trance?
Love's insubordinates gathered into a tight cluster.
Confidence waved to us.
Delicacies were created from unblemished moments.
Our own excuses were picked apart.
We prayed for pureness.
The past has had a price tag where gentle love lives.
Trust is an invisible bridging.
It can seal each touch.
Extinguishable, modified, and indecipherable –
pledges remain.
Your laughter was heard through the decades.
Phrases were stapled to my heart.
I could feel the fine print pressing against my flesh.
My declaration was without an asterisk.

Dialogue with Goddesses

A faint galaxy grew brighter.
Evening's passion was revealed.
A morning snuggle against your silkiness completes me.
Love is anywhere our daylight takes us.
For it is where you are.
You are the romantic spice – the flavor.
You are my treasury of texture and spirit.
You are my entire dream sequence.
You are my eternity.
Your whisper in my ear allows smiles to unfold.
The flare of your eyebeams takes my breath.
Love happened – without being coaxed.
Songs found in my heart were well-employed.
You gave them relevance – and accomplishment.
I was bemused by the dialogue with Goddesses.
I never thought I'd find you again.

The Score Is Even

This evens it out – in some outrageous way.
You didn't love me – you left.
I didn't love you.
I was glad you left.
Game, set, match!
Break a tackle – touchdown.
Slide – home run.
Kick – goal!
My uniform is still clean.
The score is even.

Wine Sidewalk

A broken bottle splattered, then seeped slowly,
until it wept no more.
If you must leave,
allow the love I have for you to pour into your future.
It can spill over and drown my lyrics – if you wish.
Diligent sorrow complicated us –
it lurked beside our breathless dance of passion.
Your shout falls across my destiny
and wrestles with the dried and lovely mementoes.
Wine stains are drawings on a cement canvas.
Layers of foot traffic become distressed oracles.
The scent of life happening blends with wine's bold flavor.
Solitude is sometimes the tragedy of left-behind prayer.
Crashing, glass splintered and sprayed
against a concrete concert.
Tears enticed the clouds to simper without resistance.
And I wanted you – as if I'd misplaced myself.
Wonder sways, and then hesitates
until rain makes wine flow again.

Unclaimed Romance

How can we forfeit *us* – we can't.
Or course you are the center of my existence.
I cherish the tenderness of you.
I treasure the tranquility of you.
Please stay –
so that we have one another when daylight opens.
Don't leave –
I want to be together when twilight dims.
When you're away, loneliness resonates in memories.
A naked composition forms all that is important to me.
For my happiness is authored by your eye sparkles.
You shroud the hurt from becoming mine.
Your design is the map of my yearning.
Desire surrounds me –
I long for the touch of you.
When your kiss leaves my lips,
romance evacuates the area.
Silent footprints then waltz across my soul.
Difficulties attempt to overwhelm us – they can't.
I don't want to be anywhere in life where you're missing.
You polish my world with a high gloss image
of your loveliness.
You present me with the pleasure
of your admirable qualities.
Your heat is the flame that flares within my passion.
Lift me to your embrace –
allow me to elevate you to mine.
Lean into my caress –
nearer my heartbeat.
Please allow me to clasp you throughout eternity.
Together we stay –
for you are the magnification of kindness.
Strengthen me with your hands of perfect wisdom.
Stabilize me with your smile that is sent to only my heart.
You are my humor, my warmth,
and the intensity of my spirit.

With delicacy we balance one another's exhilaration.
You are my divining expression of all that is honorable.
You are the sweep of beauty within my future.
We are the version of all –
you are my 'lover-crush' sweetheart.
We are one another's conscience,
and one another's guardians.
We tumble together as magic locates our relished
rhapsody.
We crave each electrified kiss;
we adore each sensual hot hug.
Our promise reaches the outskirts of this galaxy.
Our vow is so sturdy that no power on earth
can twist it from us.
Our belonging is so complete
that tomorrow takes us with it.
Ours is a gentle destiny.
Your love is the prized souvenir of my visit on earth.
I shall be yours until time wears me away –
then beyond.
We are for all times –
our love will belong to no other.
We are inevitable.
We were not meant to become
an unclaimed romance.

Savored Security

Security is savored.
I am cosseted by your love and you are by mine.
Other objectives are inadmissible in comparison.
For we've eliminated the structures that are insecure.
Without belonging – we are rudderless.
Our truest authenticity is inside cheer.
We bring it for one another to bask in brightness.
Darkness is a felonious commission
of time without visibility.
Yet not when we're together.
For a night with you is furnished with a burst of majesty.
When the heart is the viewer – all is possible.
Our restlessness is quelled by the touch of life.
We are tucked gently within when we discover home.
If we are self-designated – there is ecstasy's beauty.
We nestle and are well-fortified.
Love implicates us.

Trail of Perfume

What is she all about?
Who is she and what passion houses within her?
Does she strut like a drum majorette?
Are her come-hither glances from a biting ferret?
Does she shout to the moonlight?
Is there permafrost covering her heart?
Is her soul encased within a cardboard carton?
All love eventually collides with answers.
Until then, dating is a high-speed chase.
Flirtation is a hunch.
Examining the shadow that falls across her light – a guess.
She is the visitor your soul barely notices.
Her skin may be smooth, but her eyes are frozen.
Her laughter may be hearty, but does she sit upon
misery's lap?
If positive knowledge was simpler – I would tell you.
If certainty was more succinct – I would confess.
All that is left is a lingering trail of perfume.

My Flower Woman

Blossoms dangled from her hair and
swayed with her dance.
Her halo shimmered like a floral shrine.
With a friendly approach,
she taught me the language of woman.
I memorized it so I would always know it by heart.
Her glistening full lips played with mine.
Amethyst eyes mesmerized with softened flares.
Fluttering ribbons converted to elegant streamers.
Arrhythmic heartbeats sloshed their way
to my nervous twitch.
I wanted my Flower Woman's love.
The sound of nymphs singing hadn't interrupted us.
Life's glitz and ruffles weren't going
to make love a lifetime's work.
Between the trellises,
tea roses and twilight became our ceiling.
She wanted my love.
We both realized searching and finding
came in many varieties.
And absolutes were never written
into romance's instruction books.
Those days taught me life's routine is fragile.
Promises from my Flower Woman
became lovely memories.

Snugly

Slowly waking crocus lifted to our view.
In rows they opened with great emancipation –
with rivalry to be the finest.
On occasion a feral bulb would sprout away
from its designated spot.
Planting goes awry,
and we noticed a single flower.
You told me it was vulnerable and alone.
I explained it hadn't planned to be away
from its original bulb clump.
It was not mischievous.
As well-behaved as any other,
it had merely pressed itself in solitary soil.
Perhaps water had given it a shove.
It was alive now, so no matter.
My lover and I both wondered -
would that flower exist as snugly as the others?
We laughed – perhaps it was a joyous hermit.

Almost Kindred

With a gregarious mask, my lonely soul set out.
I'd never canvassed the graffiti written inside my breast.
Postponed until now, I've been enfeebled.
In darkness my spirit longed for a ritual of belonging.
Served with garish humor,
and a side of smiles, life seemed an exemplar fraud.
We admit to sharing platonic gibberish.
The exploitation of vanity intermingled with our affair.
I'd existed in a private universe – I'd barricaded love.
You felt it, but it wasn't about my love for you.
I never smothered romance – only emotions.
Economized were my words of reassurance.
Censorship hid my feelings.
I'd given you the wrong measurements of myself.
We were both chroniclers of misdirected signals.
My infractions were taken as a catalogue of contempt.
I believed your presentation an enlivened invisibility.
What a paranoid masquerade.
There was capricious egotism.
Forlorn, I comprehended only impenetrable heartache.
You said you required more of me.
My soul laments yesterday's confusion.
Inscribed deeply in my heart was lingering romance.
Love's desperation dies by inches.
If only I had believed in our embrace.
Almost kindred, we were.

Expulsion of Love Is an Obscenity

Youth was my brash accomplice.
Pride escorted me along the corridor of flirtation.
Nostalgia is a ridiculous postscript.
It required the multiplicity of Goddesses.
Rendezvous charm authenticated us both.
Intrigue was bequeathed to us
when awaiting our enchantress.
It takes a lifetime to discover the prophecy
of being let down.
Being on time for loyalty
is an ambitious challenge.
How alone might one become?
When expulsion happens,
it becomes an insightful obscenity.

Finding Her

Finding her among the recollections seemed impossible.
Sometimes love was traumatic;
other times it was tranquil.
Once in a while it was insatiable.
We pounced; we writhed.
We hid our intentions; we revealed our essence.
Our hearts were jovial and outrageous.
Subliminal messages were read by passionate eyes.
Love amused us.
It can be chaste; it can be audacious.
It can be indignant, calculating, and annoying.
It is to be found in the office, on the arcade, in the bars.
It is located along mountain trails, beaches, or in
bedrooms.
It takes on the solidity of granite,
yet it is soft as early moss.
It is luridly eternal; it is perishable.
Love is a catalyst for neurotic souls.
Love is a tonic for sudden infatuation.
Dwelling within the core of voyeurism,
it is sometimes a revelation.
It can be void of caresses;
it can be irrepressible sensuality.
It can be inebriated;
it can be sober.
It can be nurtured;
it can be starved.
Patronizing – sincere; catastrophic or tender, love is.
Mostly love is simply finding *her*.

Remembering Our Youth

Our emissaries arrived.
They wore crowns of energy.
No one at the ballpark wore petticoats.
And we listened carefully for revealing sound-bites.
Ah, romantic myths had ahold of our gloves,
as we cheered for the home team.
The shortstop taught masturbation
by one's own verbiage.
Lies were funny, but never distilled.
The pitcher's confession was a homerun,
claimed the outfielder.
Crushes were never stymied, deliberated upon,
or well-thought out,
according to the catcher's creed.
Those in the bleachers, or beneath them,
knew the reality.
Our intrinsic enslavement to the hierarchy
kept us coming back.
We bypassed the male henchmen –
they sat on the sidelines.
They waited to see if our boobs bounced.
We fluttered them only for our teammates.
We sought a truth we rarely understood.
There was a burden of plausibility.
I sought you out.
I wanted splendid remembrances of you.
Years later,
I would have your smiling photo processed in my mind.
You are in my file called Remembering Our Youth.

Our Manifesto

Our manifesto was more of a mania-feast-o.
We'd written it.
Then it was lost as it scattered.
Just as the colored glass in a kaleidoscope's top –
it rearranged as we aged.
Years, like the great torrent
of a waxing and waning moon,
sped away.
Through existence we learned more about discrepancies.
Exemplified in our ears was the sound
of sweet lyrics glowing.
Laughing, we grasp buoyant happiness.
Lifelines they were – those snickers
They demanded we know each moment
from the inside out.
We stumbled over impediments.
Before the *right* woman arrived,
we'd settled a time or two.
There was plenty of rhapsodizing to go around.

Still, sometimes surrounding our community
were people infected with bigotry.
Some played *god* games to rearrange our thinking.
Sure there was imploding deception.
Straights were mostly a tough audience.
But we held hands anyway.
Ah, chilling.
Propaganda, but no matter –
we continued cuddling.
Malice was there, but never understood.
Yet our malleable souls knew intolerance instinctively –
knew it by heart.
Under the pavilion of sedition,
we reluctantly swore to survive.
Volatile, and fanatic,
we depended on comic relief.

The merriments of our own manifesto
waited for the fracas to die down.
Our fight for equality would continue,
but never without one another.
Your kiss was worth every rope burn.
The touch of you was worth every ink stain.
Writing a manifesto is no easy act of love –
but worth every golden orgasm.

Ripples of Flesh

When my enchantress reached for me
I felt ripples, chills, and thoughts emptied.
A blithering goof?
That would be me.
Those invitations of libido excited me.
Warmth warned me of luxury
that I've never before known.
My thoughts insisted that for once,
I'd gotten it right.
Days churned and nights of passion continued.
Even my pen was placed off to the side
of hungry notebooks.
Cleared was the vacant air within my dreams.
She was before me, so life was not lackluster.
Each millisecond, each pause - belongs to us.
She still makes my skin ripple with excitement.
Chills happen within the wrap of her –
inside her arms is everything to me.
My personal enchantress still leaves me speechless.
I love her beyond all times.

Eloquence

Cascading words belong to us.
Celebratory utterances are when we share love.
We are tranquil as our hands trace each fragment.
The soft warmth of our bubbly shower
is a gentle partaking of touch.
We relish one another with each reach.
Parables bloom as if they might be floral gifts.
Loving words extol our sweetness.
Clustered are sporadic, chaining giggles.
They sprout as if they might be dripping rains.
Life is chirpy and jocular, and we become gregarious.
There is nothing supercilious, for we are profound.
There is gorgeous and decadent lovemaking.
We postpone our separations for as long as possible.
When you are away,
I await your words, warmth, and laughter.
Remembrances take me through the day and night.
For I know that this love is my life's bonus.
Our souls are not blunted,
and our joy will be recaptured.
An eloquent woman comes into one's life –
and there must be acknowledgement.
Savored, moments become eloquence.

The Vast Horizon of Age

Flirting might begin during late adolescence.
Or perhaps,
somewhere else within the vast horizon of age.
Love corroborates the heart's story.
It is exposure to the most wonderful companionship.
At the beginning, romance fuels the sensation of flesh.
Fledgling insecurities are sprayed everywhere.
We search for amorous mysticism.
No one wishes to assassinate the sweetness.
We search blueprints for tenderness.
Two people coincide to keep love safe.
That emotion becomes exquisite.
We want to learn it and we shall await its arrival.
Our smiles to one another are explicit.
Together, we create intimacies designed to be forever.
How dazzling the harbor of exhilaration is.
Crooning, canoodling, and making love
are word symbols.
The blending of bodies is the true romantic notion.
Chasing one another can run the gamut.
Time alone teaches that lesson.

Alchemist of Solitude

The alchemist of solitude grants us vanity.
We quaff up the adventurous marvel of being alone.
Quietude offers visibility to the spirit.
It links us to both adversity and promise.
Generosity is deeply imbedded within self-delusion.
Sometime it saves us – our symptoms grant clues.
When our glance bolts to the interior,
we are allowed to waltz with empathy and compassion.
We become the enthusiasts for the culture of all.
We pack our minds with themes of intent.
Seated in the lap of nature, we are inspired.
Stones are jewels becoming interior decoration.
The genius of accomplishment is swapped for ego.
Alone we find that our technique is the thread of love.
We stitch ourselves to it
when we know who we might be.
A soul's depth embodies no active exhibition.
Without labels we can still know who we are.
Ephemeral spirits present themselves.
Moments when time is our own
approach us when we're alone.

Unfolding Thought

Our upholstered brains still seem vulnerable.
We flaunt our self-absorption.
But I share my thoughts with her.
Dreams are not hidden away with stutter-steps.
Nothing between us is filtered out.
Diluted depression, indulgent shortcomings –
all the normal stuff – we know.
We are all frightened of failure.
You know I would fall twice if I lost her.
Once for each of us.
She is beguiling, and her reach swamps my reason.
She's entered my mind's cottage of contentment
where plans seek their utopia.
My lover has talked me away to foreign lands.
We've loaned out wisdom to one another.
That lifts us from isolated quests.
Vows cheer one another on.
Desire becomes our shared conspiracy.
We are both afflicted with sustaining curiosity.
Sorting, pressing, and thrusting
across our brain's pathway
leads us to the discovery.
Webbed beneath reflective currents – is love.
Complex, throughout the acres of words,
we located one another.
I love more than her magnificent presentation.
It was her unfolding thought I fell in love with first.

Roadster

I

It was a trifling matter.
Squealing tires collided with a spray of gravel.
Stones dinged a fender as our new roadster sped.
The dangerous auto had passed me.
I felt free of its threat.
A floral bouquet shifted
from the passenger's seat to the floor.
I couldn't wait to see you.
I wanted to show you our prismatically-formed rainbow.
Through those colors we viewed one another's souls.
At the behest of an enchanted Angel,
we became one another's followers.
I wanted your hands to hold my heart.

II

My great fortune was to present you
with an armload of spraying of daisies,
roses and carnations.
And the key to our luxury roadster dangled –
teasing you to take your first drive in our new roadster.
My heart filled with joy as I sat on the passenger's side.
There was pride in both of us
when you slid into the driver's seat.
With aplomb, you took the wheel,
and soon we were back on the highway.
A rainbow chase would take us there.
How loved by me you have always been, I whispered.
Words were barely out,
when you swerved.
Suddenly, that vehicle of bigotry was seen.
Its brand name was hatred.
I'd warned you before how they reviled us.
With mutual recriminations, the race was on.
You pumped the accelerator.
With debauchery, they yielded.

Then the sordid game
turned into beating hearts and jangled nerves.
The verdict was seconds away.
We lamented the probable crash with somber eyes.
Love gave us words of clarity –
yet they seemed barren.
The menacing vehicle's headlights blinded us.
For our last moments, a frozen kiss –
was stamped upon our lips.
I clutched you.
Your flesh found its way into my embrace.
Our Angel was in partial view.
We were suddenly pulled over by the word of sacrifice.
Our bright red roadster had been contaminated.
But it was not the embezzler of our lives.
Our backseat Angel came into full view.
An arch of pastel colors had saved us.

Where We Are

Our enchantress seeks me, finds me, and comforts me.
Who can ask for more?
The smoothness of her fingers against my smiling face –
well, that is only a hint.
When I am in her embrace, I realize where we are.
We are within the state of love.
We are where we must be, and wish to be.
Our very preamble casts us across this vista of time.
Her kiss protects me from uncertainly.
It is a perfect kiss – instinctual and complete.
She empowers us all.
Qualms about being brave enough to face the future –
they go from where we are.
We make love
and that is where we are.

.

Part Two
Soft Side

	Page
Soft Side	32
Custom Kindness	33
LoveShip	34
A Season's Story	35
Glancing Back at a Fear of Love	36
Lighthearted Yesterday	37
Her Softness	40
Selfless	41
Tamed	42
Send for Me	43
Romance Ends	44
Underside of Softness	46
My Lady's Bravery	47
Verses	49
The Good Times Rolled	50
Vowed	51
Kiss Time	52
She Gave a Damn	53
If Love Were to Dissolve	54
My Tab	55

Soft Side

On the soft side of a poem,
Like the shelter of a home,
Where the touch is partly reach,
Where the mountains meet the beach.

Your words bring me very near.
Even though you can't be here.
Lyrics rest upon our lips
As I kiss your fingertips.

You are here within my song
Where you've been so very long.
In your eyes I dream romance
As you wrap me in our dance.

Trading grins and outstretched hands,
Trekking hills and waltzing sands,
Like hugging sunshine in the rains,
Our deep longing still remains.

On the sweet side of a smile,
We're together all our while.
Love's been worth my longtime wait
Guess it's time to trust my fate.

Custom Kindness

Enchanted, I was compelled to
desire your custom kindness.
Yet, I expected to see you wave goodbye.
I pressed softly against your tenderness.
Kisses slipped from your lips.
Touches swiveled slowly.
Bliss grew in my head and crowded my thoughts.
Melodies were gusty sounds surrounding us.
When I envisioned *us* –
the world went saucy and sweet.
I reached for you.
My voice tightened.
Skies were silky charcoal drawings.
They became blue wings of my heaven –
stretching across a blinking horizon.
My soul was both drafty and noisy - before you.
The burrows of earth were dented and frayed –
until you.
I sought kindness – and you customized it.
I have always wanted you.

LoveShip

As with friendship,
only beginning an intense love –
our LoveShip was special.
Blossoms wrangled their way into service.
They flirted –
showing their colors to attract bees.
They wanted pollination.
Scents were the attractions.
Lovers bloom.
I see your friendship.
Desiring the conversion – I'll flirt.
I'll wear a palette's color scheme.
Whatever it takes for you to love me –
I'll do that.
And much more.

A Season's Story

That season was lonely as I glanced aside.
Removing our hurt was again tried.
To return to sender, with my best regard,
I made life a year-round greeting card.

That season was painful 'til I reached toward
An unbuttoned heart where I'd stored
Our drifting memories with each defamed word.
From two vantages points, it would occur.

That season was harsh, yet I added mirth in.
I set grief aside and would begin.
Stomping anger, I doused the raging flames out.
Embers tell what the season's about.

I tallied fineness, sans material wealth.
There was love, and each day of good health.
Life is poetry, art, and music I've heard.
I was grateful for each kindly word.

It wasn't the season's fault – that was unfair.
With counting blessings – I'd had my share.
I knew the importance of looking ahead.
Each story's path is where I'll be led.

Glancing Back at a Fear of Love

Our emotional blend is fatal.
I'd once remarked that
struggling and loneliness are preferable.
For love is a simpering socialite –
invited, yet not fully appreciated.
Willing to sample Sappho – we find our home.
But it was fondness,
in the company of eroticism,
that reminded us to trust.
As we swapped coming-out stories,
we'd tried to consolidate them.
The essence of love was our continuation.
Belief is a portion of optimism.
For caring had always been
encouraged by a circlet of time.
It would orbit nearer,
but was never as I'd hoped.
I glanced at the moon and squinted at the sun.
Asking the universe why relationships terminate
becomes a throwaway question.
Understanding another's love
is as difficult as knowing your own.
A friend once contended that romance was heart jazz.
Sensuality meets with the soft center, and is all.
I'd once heard the sound of loneliness.
I was that noise of heartbreak.
My eyes had closed like metal clamps.
Now my song was reassurance.
Jubilance prompted my best lyrics.
My eyes were opened –
for I could laugh, and smile.
And no one was frightened – only loved.

Lighthearted Yesteryear

All aboard for yesteryear land.
If you wish to go, please take my hand.
We'll wander along to distant treasure.
We'll journey back to homespun pleasure.
Close your eyes,
dream of skies
blue and clear,
have no fear.
You're the captain of your ship.
And off we'll go on our little trip.
Hang on tight
with all your might.
We're going right
to see the sight.
Huge balloons and candy canes,
sugar dolls on gumdrop lanes.
Kids on parade
drink pink lemonade.
Bright blue bicycles
race gleaming red tricycles.
Hop aboard a merry-go-round.
Listen to the hurdy-gurdy sound.
A Jumping Jack
has licorice in a sack.
A tiny red fox
plays in a sand box.
With candy bars
and toy cars,
and a kaleidoscope for color's design,
and a giggle says that all is fine.
Animal crackers eat jelly beans.
Lollypop signs point to silly scenes.
Inside castles there are kings and queens
celebrating Christmases and Halloweens.
We'll have great times in the place I know.
We're all captains and we can all row

across the sea of make-believe we'll go.
With court jesters, and acrobats
we'll all wear special funny hats.
Hoist away, spread the sails.
We shall wait for husky gales.
They'll float our ship across the blue.
We'll travel ever and ever anew.
When we arrive at our own special land
we'll wiggle our toes in glittering sand.
There will be gifts galore
inside a huge toy store.
We'll hear music and song
and know we belong.
Here comes the cake,
hear the squeals we'll make.
Now comes the shakes, malts, and soda pop.
If we spill, whoops, here comes the mop.
Candy will sprinkle out of the sky.
Paper airplanes swirl as they fly.
Chocolate, gingersnaps, and laughing we are.
We'll charge up a mountain to touch a star.
After all, it isn't that high.
Not if we reach and really try.
We'll run in the meadow, and climb a hill.
We'll eat Cracker Jacks until we get our fill.
We'll jump and run, then waltz with the sun.
When night has come and day is done,
we'll wander on home and hop in our beds.
We'll pull up the covers and then the spreads.
Tucked into bed by kind, gentle hands
we'll return to our own special lands.
We'll wake blurry-eyed to wait for our friends.
And we'll travel around twisting bends.
Back to our place,
we'll hasten to race.
Hear the train coming, clickedy-clack –
coming down the well-worn track.
It will pick us up to take us shipside.

We'll ready our departure to take a ride.
There are flowers with colors all aglow.
The hills ahead spread like a huge rainbow.
We'll pluck new petals each as they bloom
from a magical flower in our playroom.
Childhood is bright as all the sun's rays.
So let's recall the best of our sweet days.
A childhood with love and without fear
is the best kind of lighthearted yesteryear.

Her Softness

My woman finds me in the dark.
Her softness holds each portion of my skin at once.
Within a luscious wrap,
I hear her laughter that spurts lyrically
across our night.
I locate her behind tears that I've wiped away.
I promise no sorrow
would dare impoverish our lives.
Not when our solace has bound us together.
Some subliminal hint finds her
each time she leaves my side.
Her beguiling frown, so elusive, is part of her spirit.
Her grin visits my grateful soul.
Our hug is warmth against my body.
When she calls my name – I'm with her.
She lights up my dreams –
until her those dreams
became illusionary, threadbare hopes.
Her soft walnut-colored hair falls loosely
on her shoulders,
then on mine.
Recollections are never worn away,
for she clutches me tightly.
Wrapped in arms that provide home, she keeps me.
Each kiss takes my lips on her journey.
Her mouth is adventure.
Her eyes are a path, and her smile is a journey.
Enchantment lifts us
as we are assimilated into the miracle.
Our fashion of flesh emerges in the dark.
Her softness locates me.

Selfless

Selflessness is tender as a scented geranium.
It enriches us both.
Happiness is our duet.
Just as the flower's fragrances
invite butterflies to land,
you draw me near with your sweet fresh bouquet.
We grasp tightly and form our lives together.
As if we're finches in a thicket, we snuggle.
Nature is idyllic, we believe.
We inspect surrounding oak groves.
Birds perch on the silhouettes of limbs.
They twill, whir, and chirp.
We chat as we trek
through daybreak's chalky grayness.
Washed skies have drained throughout the night.
Torrents of morning's hushed rain
doused the vegetation.
Clods of earth have become soggy soil.
We tread carefully along the path.
Our roster is never indifferent.
For we allow love to escort us.
We tightly seal our hearts to a sweet cadence.
We encourage romance,
and allow intersecting –
until we are unified.
Our lullaby is a simple sequence.
Wisdom is stretched to capacity.
There is more longing with each nanosecond.
Capturing the floral balminess, chronicling wildlife,
and cataloguing nature
is something we want for one another.
Sharing – it assures certainty for our belonging.
We'll remain together –
gifting one another mornings.
We point out finches, clouds, geraniums, oak groves,
and all else that poses as splendor.
That requires two selfless hearts.
Thank you for yours, and I give you mine.

Tamed

The taming of love's sensory receptors has begun.
I reach and you've stayed through the darkness.
Words burn,
before they cool to the universe's temperature.
Wisdom requires emotional magic and manacles.
Indelible prisms glide across our hands.
On a pale day, we wait for intimacy.
Your winsome charm is auto-pilot romance.
The depth of us caresses edges.
Our stellar dream bypasses gimmickry.
A kiss of spiritual embodiment begins us.
Treasury is complete after morphing.
We travel from intricate, to introspective,
and finally to sublime.
Your expressions are cushions.
Your inflection registers with my anticipation.
Palpitation of your pulse is in sync with mine.
Our skin resonates with trembling nerves.
Your eye-smile searches the image of me.
Expressive, your glance brightens mine.
Your lips indulge me.
Their dreams graze upon mine.
We need no reservation
when giving one another *us*.
We never withhold, we never are uncertain.
Pledged - we are hearts given freely.
I have never given so much, and asked so little.
I ask that you love me, as you are taming me.

Send for Me

Send for me when you have
a question about my warmth.
Silence has always staked me to a portion
of the heart unknown to others.
I hide out during storms.
I've learned to dissect smiles.
For it is believed that one should not smile
at a snarling dog.
Animals believe we are baring our teeth at them.
I've learned to read eyes that present each word
before it is said.
I know the shrug,
I understand the flippant arrogance.
Provocation puts me on high alert.
Send for me when you have a question
about my softness.
I'll tell you how it pains me
to see unkindness and hatred.
I shall not smile,
nor shall I allow the story in my eyes to be told.
Send for me if you require my answers.
I am warm and I am soft
because there is love within me.
How simple can it be?

Romance Ends

I
Romance ends
when ancient ghosts overtake wonder.
Rattling within, inside of time, is a cameo.
That lovely woman guided me.
Pulses beat their own sound.
Cataclysmic snarls flirted with us both.
I had searched my merit system.
Your soul was struggling as much as mine was.
What grizzled heartache is left behind
when an affair ends?
Introspection sets down the ground rules.
What solemn barriers make us become stray souls?
We'd peeled away layers of altruistic thoughts.
Chords of memory extolled the fossilized music.
Giggles appeared
from behind our naked cover-up.
We were investigators devoted to the fringe.
We'd made love in the courtyard,
and then we hid out.
We stacked firewood
so that our bonfire would be seen.
Coals were singed by our unhappiness.
Searing heat addressed us with sadness.
It had melted the goodness away.
We were spun from the seduction of Angels.
A clap of heaven's anger became a battle cry.
Our remedy was a collapsing fragrance of desire.
A theologian's seed had created us.
Mingling with a fallen Goddess
was our comeuppance.
What emblazoned manacles we had unearthed.
We'd crawled through the festival.
We'd petitioned one another for answers.
We'd become crushed chalk –
our voice became sightless.

We were travelers in a game
that had filed us away.
I had no veneration for those who'd defiled us.
Euphoria was our gold-framed patron.
Romance has left the building

II
Billowing and festering
were the horizontal missteps.
We vaulted the arroyo,
only to fall into a raging sonata.
We snuck under a black robe of midnight.
The raiding party had invaded our tragedy.
Our pseudonym steamed
beneath the underground prison.
Shadows spread and frailty called our names.
My voice tip-toed in.
Her scream burned my eyelids.
Throwaway laughs screeched.
We never found who bit into the cake first.
Such rich, pink frosting!
Luggage was crammed full of glory.
Humanity seemed catalogued in guilt.
Debt has beheaded gluttony.
Feathers split as we pulled our shawl near.
We seemed so awkward.
When romance falls apart,
darkness bites into our flesh.
I had trusted her with my love.
She'd convinced me
that we were one another's light.
We ignited all that once mattered.
Life had mockingly intruded with its reality.
Now I'm glad I meant nothing to her.
The ghosts are welcome to my share of nothing.

Underside of Softness

Betrayal distorted her claim of concern.
Our public image was not a reliable source.
The comfy tributes had taken a windsurfing ride.
Oak rocking chairs were never exhibits of tomorrow.
She issued her disclaimer.
For one delirious day we were both bargains.
She'd awarded random grins and drowsy eyes.
I turned down franchise sex.
I don't like downcast eyes
that are mildewed and somber.
I evacuated her den –
it was an exhaustive effort.
Fresh scowls took the place of fake smiles.
It was all concluded –
the underside of softness ceased.
There was no fix-up available for hypocrisy.
Lethal doses of squabbles stumbled to a halt.
Missing particles formed resentment.
Love had become a silly animation.
There, I've said it again.

My Lady's Bravery

How could I trust again?
She was at my side, with her softness.
And all I could say was that love had hurt me.
Sharp edges were petrous caresses.
I would remember them always.

Deep down I had known the rules of my emotions.
Tranquility provides more orgasms
than chaos ever furnished.
A gasp of love is a sound
more explanatory than words.
Theory leaps over the voices when sex invades.
The elucidator of our human essence is required.
Moonlight spills across our side of the globe.
I'd just experience the turmoil
of an accretion disk.
Romance had stomped my spirit.

But my Lady arrived to lift me away from lechery.
Our lips traced the ambiance of one another.
Hug clusters began our excursion.
Tangled bed linens were our mattress artwork.
The bed was our prop.
Laughs rose musically, simultaneously, and tenderly.
We grazed on thoughts of what came next.
The temperature warmed as we tethered.
We were absorbed.

I allowed emotional entanglements to sear my soul.
Our eyes shut tightly
as the smoldering embrace startled us.
Urgency converted the ravenous desire.
Glistening skin heated; circulating hips pressed;
throbbing bosoms swelled,
and we were certainly courageous.
The banquet became an oscillating orgasm.

Damp surrender allowed a quenching rest.
Love's intensity was a cherished rhapsodic frolicking.
Arousal comforted us as we nestled.
My thoughts became bundles of unopened folders.
We rested against one another's doubt.
I could always trust my brave Lady.
She's taken a chance
on my recovery from unsweetened love.

Verses

We searched for the songs we sang.
Those lyrics wanted to see who was behind the door.
Staying in tune,
the verses had wired themselves to each other.
Although they'd walled one another inside,
music lifted.
Although they'd placed a thick roof over our ballads,
their beat could be heard.
The pitch of love was circular,
and as oval as life itself.
Pleasure was a textile we celebrated.
Emotions dropped as the walls crumbled inward.
The meter grabbed the fence below.
Fortissimo woke us.
We picked the lock of rhythmic duets.
Each latch added another opening chorus.
We visited affectionate sounds.
Glimmering dreams resounded.
The band framed a happy ending for us.
Yet we knew a quest doesn't end
by being found or finding.
There is always one more hidden lyric.
There is always another verse.

The Good Times Rolled

Back in the day,
we were equipped with our cave spirit.
We clothed ourselves in bright garments
to be safe.
Today was our friend.
We were one another's comfort.
Yesterday was the neighbor
we called ourselves.
For with youthfulness comes the unknown.
Romance came and went.
We didn't belong to the earth, sea, or sky.
Our starlight was often away.
When we gathered – happiness renewed us.
I held stray women and they held me.
Laughter bound us tightly.
Sometimes their faces sprinkle
in front of my memory.
We were refugees no more.
When a smile offered its promise
music lit up the dancefloor.
We held one another until morning arrived.
Still hearing the congregation of songs,
and seeing the roving lighting above,
we shared friendship.
Women allowed the good times to roll.
We kissed because sometimes
touch is all that proved we were alive.

Vowed

We vowed to never set one another aside.
For it is in her arms I find safety,
and forever.
All those years ago we consoled one another
with trite pillow talk.
We lounged on damp grass,
and felt it drying beneath us.
We still told one another
everything will be fine.
We finagled blurbs
of amorous sweetness back then.
Pure charm is still in our words.
Our collaboration binds us, and protects us.
When we said exclusive, we meant it.
We never want to leave one another's side
in the morning – or any other time.
We banter that there can't be *insinuations* of love.
It's got to be real – just as it has always been.
I still lose my breath when she speaks.
We don't blather
about platitudes and pulsating carnality.
There was our prattle
that exonerated ribald humor.
Laughter keeps us immune from dainty jargon.
We live in homespun sketches.
I want her every moment of the day,
every way of every moment.
Our tender vernacular matched all our promises.
We had once articulated
our desire to remain together.
We couldn't live without one another.
Goodbye would treat our hearts badly.
It's a word we never want to feel.
The word *together* is our friend.
Our oath was living's preamble.
Love never ends;
nor do vows that exit the heart.

Kiss Time

We kiss one another awake.
You whisper to me as if your words are being sung.
We don't want our romance to wear out.
Our heartbeats are wearing fancy costumes.
It's a time of late frost.
Wrens and robins have invited blossom.
For it is kick-off for a season of blooms.
Boughs of lacey green hang across our path.
Endurance is a precious energy.
Yes, our sensual souls flicker and flutter.
We don't impersonate great screen lovers.
Our own clarity is warm enough.
I trace the lines of your body,
kissing each inch with lips of longing.
My once empty bed
is now filled with amazement.
Mellow kisses are savory
as they take me to where you are.
Even when you're not with me –
you seem to be.
I visualize – with eyes closed.
My knees quiver with the thought of you.
My eyes throw sparks a million miles.
I feel the brush of our lips.
We are both starving for sunshine.
The purpose of delicacy
is located on the meadow lands.
I desire you in our bed of tangled wildflowers.
Tenderness surrounds me.
I await a weekend of kiss time with you.

She Gave a Damn

She was a woman who gave a damn.
It was springtime,
and she was moving to the coast.
When we met – I was awe-inspired by Susan.
She had been bereft –
yet she was resigned.
She always took up the offer
to peer into another's heart.
Susan never saw the corner place
where weeping begins.
She always sought the hidden place
where laughter starts.
Life was relaxed,
and she repaired hurt and anger.
Admitting that she was questing after wisdom,
Susan delved meaning.
Her life was a fluke of some torrential nature.
Or so she claimed with the cover of laughter.
Stars are giant rotating jewels
that swing around us on cue.
According to Susan,
we are all mystified by the night sky.
Worlds are bright specks – adrift –
just as we are.
There were no theories and formulas
she didn't lust to know.
She grasped at enlightenment.
She stopped to look
through the cracks of all gates.
When parties began, she kicked off her shoes.
Her ritual never ended –
she announced
that pheromones spread as she danced.
She never looked back through her history.
But she gave a damn –
and she once told me she loved me.

If Love Were to Dissolve

What would we do if love were to dissolve?
Character witnesses would
stop watching wild adventures.
Ghosts and saints would pick over the bones.
Craggy earth would become dust.
Entire lives would be harnessed beneath hardship.
Humanity has toiled – it would all be lost.
Some would be derailed and seduced
with bogus promises.
They would be too tired for love to begin –
only tawdry moments of sex.
Hustlers staggered along without fear.
Life became deliberate.
As if living on a faraway outpost,
there was no road home.
No one could find love's remnants.
No one could discover their way home.
No one would vouch for one another.
Regrettably, earth's trenches were filled.
Ties had been broken.
Those standing nearest the searchlights
were sacrificed first.
Pollsters had been mistaken.
Love was not unsavory.
And it didn't need to be dissolved.

My Tab

I've had fun settling my tab with life.
And am having fun - yet.
Looking back,
I realize how wonderfully unpredictable women are.
They are strong and fragile.
They are fraudulent and loyal.
They are strident and harmonious.
They are venomous and affectionate.
Along the path, there were flimflam artists.
Some were enjoyable – a couple not so much.
I never turn my life over to boredom.
There have been misfits along the way –
a few times I was the misfit.
My life has covered some silly referendums.
I've recovered nicely.
Not one woman left my spirit completely battered.
I've never been an experiment –
nor have I treated any woman as an experiment.
Affairs were often historical –
and sometimes hysterical.
There have been uncontested charges –
even a smattering of besotted, smitten verse.
My self-advice gets simpler with each year.
Forever is a very long reach.
I know that because I'm out of date.
But for the record – I've settled my tab.

Part Three

Divas

	Page
Glitzy Swagger	58
Broken Moment	59
Diva's Along the Way	60
Awakening with Her	61
Sugar-Coated Heart	62
Diva, Babe	64
The Unkind Affair	65
Corseted Loitering	66
My Roguish Egalitarian	68
Meeting in a Bar	70
Quiet and Solitude	71
Strangers Doing the Honors	72
Ancient and Eternal	73
Syllables	74
Motion for Discovery	76
Flawed	77
Winter's Swanish Lovesong	78

Glitzy Swagger

I admire your glitzy swagger.
With elegant femininity –
you still got sway goin' on.
In my mind,
you are an epochal Goddess of delight.
We intersected and shared precious time.
Mild and sweet you are,
yet you can reboot to a sledgehammer's slam.
Quirky, you excavate laughter with precision.
When you hold me in your arms,
your gentleness elevates me greatly.
Your kiss of passion electrifies my soul.
Your wild heart clarifies my love.
I have never felt passed over when we near.
With all of your glitzy swagger,
you are always our show's star.
But I'm the one who still feels special.

Broken Moments

Ushered away,
were the moments of her.
She slid across the universe –
leaving me alone.
My world emptied out.
My broken moments would heal –
as they must.
Of course, I want to share her life.
I'm designed for romance.
My heart has never been sealed –
nor has it been dubious.
Moments are always repairable.
We've refused to discard our feelings.
Patches, glue guns, baling wire, epoxy –
sweet words, and smiles.
I'll be there too.

Diva's Along the Way

Fulfilled by the Divas of Lesbos,
my life has praised their glorious altar.
Serenades tumbled,
and some affairs stumbled,
but somehow we remained fearless souls.
We dialed into our relish of existence.
This journey was without strategy.
For preplanning was a mischievous glare.
Frowns were for plans that might go wrong.
We were never bland categories.
Our coterie gladdened a harmonious world.
Experiences added up to mellow remembrances.
Rocketing through our own turbulence got us there.
For each precious Diva sculpted harps
and sang lullabies.
They also explored the vocal chords.
Achievements were flamboyant lyres.
And the laughter of lovely women was flavored.
Regrets were choking bellows,
yet were understood and accepted.
The choir lifted songs into the air.
Diva's along the way were enchantment.
All of our best designs had been restrung
through the spirit of womanhood.
Futuristic gifts would recast our streamlined glory.
Exalted, Divas enkindle the day's blessings.
Give me a moment,
and I'll send you a dream.

Awakening with Her

Her *signature* hot steamy embrace is lavished
with tenderness.
The cosmopolite and cowgirl
speak the same language.
Embedded souls press back a tugging magnetism.
We rarely unlock our arms.
With an introvert's exclusive desire,
I ache for her.
We are the clarity of one another
through the morning.
We trade laughter –
her quicksilver wit lampoons life.
Rhythmic chatter is never dull.
Fine-tuned are the words we chew and swallow.
For each thought is authentic,
with cognitive exploration.
When she speaks, I declare her brilliance.
I am lost in the loveliness of her.
Our memories are ribbons
trapping together the piles of words.
Within envelopes, our letters are traded.
We linger with a gold-tinted sunrise,
as it interrupts our eroticism.
Euphemisms call us sweetheart.
We know we are guest
upon this crust of a planet.
She sings an early wake-up song.
We accept the globe's maternity.
We never find morning offensive,
for love requests us.
Interpreting a Goddess's inspiration is guesswork.
Well, I have awakened to a Goddess's love.
Lyrics speak to our souls,
and we achieve our message.
We are all each one another's fragile offering.
I understand awakening with her.

Sugar-Coated Heart

Sugar-coated hearts were in abundance.
As I sat amongst the debris of my past,
I placed aside ornaments to be given to charity.
The largest heap of memorabilia was valueless litter.
It would be converted into destroyed rubbish.
Tarnished, unvarnished trophies of my past –
taken from storage, would be reassembled.
I hadn't noticed so many scratches.

Most of my belongings could be filed away
in the empty file cabinets of time.
Possessions that empty souls
required reassurance.
Mementos were to be left behind
where they might be loved.
My caresses would reach across
lacquered thrift shop counters.
Discarded emotions braced
against the angularity of lost love.
Photographs –
sweetly smiling images were fading.
No orbiting heat was ignited –
only shaded solace.
Upon greeting cards –
both bright and dull, dazzling words
printed the earth's tempo.
As if they were limbs going limp,
lyrics hobbled proudly.
Tense penmanship showed inhibitions.
Exposed and suspended, loops expressed love.

Contours of fleshy words glided
against well-sifted souls.
They'd been pelted by sensitivity –
and were long ago dismantled.
My reminiscence told of loss.
That corner of my version was prodded
throughout free-fall.

Letter openers dissected the wrappers.
Elasticity was on simulcast.
Scrolls of blazing love
were exchange across their parchment.
Ink dripped as it swore to hold us to our vows.
Draping shawls, once looped together by energy,
had become unstitched.
Trust had punctured –
additional correspondence lingered.
Jabbed were nestling pages.
Ascending words were expansion bridges.
They jutted with fragmented memories.
Reflections, too durable to dim, were sustained.

Neatly stacked were the letters I cherished.
Bound in heartbreak,
they were from the pen of one who left early.
Smudged by time and tears,
they had nearly wasted from wear atop my dresser.
They were exchanged by the spirits
of nothing and no one.
We'd been victims of the evening storm.
After she died, I searched inspiration.

A faraway gale lifted music to my heart.
Lyrics spoke to my soul, achieving a message.
Without sugar-coating
we might become one another's place
where grief dwelled.
But we are also in an area
where enchantment triumphed.
After I knew that, how could I accept false love?
Her heart was the trophy I most cherished.
Yet it had also become dented.
Perhaps it had also fallen
when eternity dropped
the heart's most fraudulent prayer.

Diva, Babe

My Diva Babe had fulfilled hopes
throughout every hollow known to woman.
We were all reaching toward
the high altar of Lesbos.
She was delicious dripping honey.
Her serenade never stumbled –
it gave me time to catch up to her.
She was a storyteller –
building stacks of written pledges.
She meant every word, so we needed be careful.
She'd dialed into my happiness.
She knew that misguided strategy
is a glare from hell.
She understood that pity is a frown from earth.
And sometimes a journey hits the sacred button.
Diva Babe knew how to alert the sensuous alarms.
My Diva Babe helped me overcome obstacles.
Coaxing and compromising,
she insisted I ignore strange paths.
Every inlet, highway, and landing strip
was without warped roads.
Each step was wonder.
A coquette's game had overtaken us both.
The route least stumbled upon
is not always correct.
Concessions lacking love aren't always failures.
This is only if one runs out of one's self to give,
she whispered.
If detachment is unkind,
we can experiment with walls – then space.
Dissolving goals, lifting fences,
and collecting sanctuaries –
are only requirements.
Diva Babe helps keep life sweeter.
Only, she insists,
if we listen to her savvy instructions.

Kieran York

The Unkind Affair

Night became a bracket holding stars from falling.
A cluster of clarity
was all the breathing space required.
A wad of simmering atmosphere
was once as bright as fireworks.
Under the weighted nothingness
came a choppy confession.
I had been love-duped.
When I inquired – more trickery trickled.
A march of lies had wounded infatuation's flavor.
Crisscrossing was a wave of nausea.
Paranoia replaced my trust with self-loathing.
I'd been hoodwinked and bashed by a storm of rubble.
An outer-edge of hell surrounded me.
Retaliation fueled her unbalanced rants.
I limped away with the heaviness of betrayal.
I would not have believed love could so quickly turn.
But it was *never* love.
It was as if the ground beneath shifted in one ugly turn.
How could I have fallen into her pit of hatred?
Did a woman's scorn really exist to this extent?
Imploding, my galaxy seemed lost.
Gazing upward –
I accepted that I also appeared lost.
There had never been such an unkind affair.

Corseted Loitering

I've come here today to discover if magic lasts.
Our corseted loitering began years ago.
Beginning with apprehension,
we felt time eluding us.
Fragments of fear and strain stuffed our minds.
Relax, and enjoy the day.
Hammocks ticked as they swayed,
and I was heated by the strong sun,
and it's reflection.
Soothed with suspension,
our bodies melded to one.
Time's Rorschach test blinked us back to reality.
Batting eyelashes and grimaces
completed my puzzle.
Conversation was bedecked
with the magnificence of us.
The spinning motion of fact had made love frail.
Expressions were gristle with appliqued smiles.
Life's sheen wrapped around my nerves,
and strung like heavy cord.
Turmoil took a tumble across a road of mystery.
One of us was in the waiting room.
One of us was having our heart extracted.
Concerns carved away all lusty reassurance.
Sensory equipment became disabled.
Boisterous impatience required
that we answer too quickly.
It was as near
as either of us came to admitting love.
Guttural laughs surfaced when our faces creased.
Achievements mended by crepe paper streamers
gave way.
Existence converted to doubt.
A nearby sprinkler bathed us in disorientation.
Oceans created a long swim.
Although dangling days strung us together,

I paused.
Sun-bleached journeys are rarely complete.
Years are heavy with infatuation.
This was my discovery,
and mine alone.

My Roguish Egalitarian

You'd unpacked your intellectualized depression
before I could cheer you.
There was no breakthrough.
Social allegory had its way with you.
We had attempted to make new toasts.
We gulped the wine of life until we gagged.
Now flames leap up and warm us.
Mellow and forever is our laughter.
Our tears are lost to yesterday.
Paradoxically,
we'd shared an aching symbolic pain.
Watching love as it poured itself away
from us was sad.
When our event began again,
love's delicacy was near.
We were aware that sipping
the ecstasy of years lost could purify us.
Knowledge wasn't a help.
Yet never knowing was a blindfold.
We maneuvered away from the feast.
We gently wiped the mist of yesterday
from one another's eyes.
We strained to make it better.
I could barely see you.
Your vocal expression wasn't to be deciphered.
Your glimpse blinked flares.
Candles were crowned with flickers.
The glowing charcoal wick was a steady orange.
We wanted the flame to remain.
Bizarre spirals of wax grew from the tabletop.
You reached and lifted
the partially melted monument.
It cracked as it was stripped from the table.
Or was it the fireplace's crackle?
Or your laugh?
The snarl of ridicule was an eerie desperation.

Too much self-censorship, we confessed.
Inherently we knew our well-structured plot.
If we were to part –
we would sob loudly.
Isolation would find us in the dark.
Thick sentences would flush
a measured ballad of soul sounds.
Our explanation would be lined with our hearts.
You didn't really want
to be a grand exhibition.
You didn't really want
to pour a waterfall of wine.
I wanted to erase the moments
when I feared losing you.
I stopped anticipating miracles –
there was only you.
My roguish egalitarian –
you were always enough for me.
Up until the day you left my side –
just as you told me you might.

Meeting in a Bar

We both ignored the steely glances
of jealous lovers.
As if they were the victims of erosion –
they quickly disappeared.
If they'd have wanted us –
they would have treated us better, you said.
My reply was that perhaps
they were being eradicated
by someone's else's smile.
Words written on eternity
became leftover tidbits.
We bake on a sweltering, orbing planet –
or inside an embrace.
We froze during the next interval of antiquity.
Glitz and razzle-dazzle
became our genetic disposition.
We'd tugged memories along with us.
Rhetoric became a fragment on our brain.
Our dialogue was a scrap of enchantment.
A strike of lightning painted our portraiture.
Love may collapse, we warned.
But our comment verifies
that we are packaged in transparency.
I knew that your hypnotic eyes mesmerized me.
Your cordial smile was intoxicating.
If there were heresies –
 they came well-hidden.
Your touch was combustible
and it targeted my heart.
Eroticism made me yearn for you.
When dancing, you became my temptress.
For a moment I believed I might open a vein for you.
Our introduction might have led
to something disposable.
Or it could regenerate the memories
we'd hugged so near to us.
Tomorrow is another epochal moment.

Quiet and Solitude

Night was as quiet as an antique grave.
She watched with intensity.
High-powered glitz
had tampered with her expectations.
My rich, crisp voice immunized her soul.
Then there was silence.
The quiet in my heart compounded.
The great shadow flashed a frame at a time –
as if words
wanted to play leapfrog for sequence.
There was a finite amount of thinking to do.
Romance's sustainability is forged by two.
Outside hurt and inside hope was downloaded.
I believed in monogamy.
Now I wondered
if it was a bedraggled, elusive myth.
So much of what is done to one another
is premeditated.
No one is promiscuous on purpose.
She believed isolation would sanitize her.
With boredom, she yawned before bellowing.
There was titillation among the nymphets.
She was seduced while on that adventure.
Betrayal was too noisy for my sensibilities.
Her new lover was called *the next in line*.
Her new home was called *partyville*.
My new lover was named Quiet.
My new home was named Solitude.

Strangers Doing the Honors

We began by avoiding one another.
Resistance was confidential and agreed upon.
Soon we were shuttling between love and hate.
Under the slight brightness of a 'cuspy' moon,
we shared our evening with wine
and a symphonic poem.
Some evenings were cool to the touch.
Others were blistering with blazing sex.
Voices lied about our heart's contents.
Expletives of justification
were in another dictionary.
Our eyes produced the same tired readouts.
We couldn't resurrect the sizzle.
What a miniscule travesty we lived.
Varnish ceased to make the difference.
We'd prolonged consideration until we realized
the quick tick of time.
It was chasing us.
I'd never forgiven you.
And I'd never understood
why you still wanted me.
You'd wanted to pretend it never happened.
You needed to pretend I still loved you.

Ancient and Eternal

Ancient and eternal
are two different locations.
The tyrannical stories
have marched through history.
They reassured companions.
The treacherous, unsanctioned pretense
has evaporated.
Forbidden poems from forgotten poets linger.
Newer notations were encumbering –
yet freshly prepared.
Life's theme existed – it knew us all.
Just as we know the caves of our predecessors.
And as we know the pale blue iris
and it's feathered soul.
Current flowed through our wild imagery.
Past inhabitants have been blotted away.
Great swaths of over-growth had hidden the horizon.
Our quest is frail – but it staggers toward reality.
The traveler's spirit is often slain.
Squandered, each moment is newborn,
and too soon ends.
We haven't grasped the definition of eternity.
Although we've searched infinity's address –
Those adventures forever eluded us.
What is left - only kindness prevailed.
What stays behind –
is love that heals and builds.
For love is never a superstition.
Ancient is lost in the past.
Eternal lives in tomorrow's empty space.

Syllables

We are all chaperones.
Or perhaps, we are custodians.
The soul's garble tells of us.
Our vocalization spins syllables.
We are top-echelon celebrities.
We begin with infancy's utterance.
Like love, speech is often ineffectual.
It's distilled through barely-developed lungs.
Human acoustics encounter a first meeting
with expression.
Ecstasy is a second contender.
It crowds against its own enamored restraint.
The delicious repository of remembrances
is next in line.
Our unedited version allows truth to seep out.
Hidden sentences become closed-captioned.
For the occupant of real understanding is trust.
How can it be otherwise?
Attempting to mollify one another won't work.
Carefully inspected word-stuff is destructive.
Thoughts are perpetual sentries.
Chaining our emotion by erasing silence is useless.
Against our melody is the wail of a propeller.
Secrets are all concepts that aren't shared.
Soft dreams keep us from becoming separated.
We feast on verbs and nouns –
as if they are our nourishment.
Sabotaged by querulous paragraphs,
comedy is short-lived.
Misspelled scruples brandish pronouns and veil us.
Forged ideals have coerced split-infinitives.
Encumbered, we are insipid spellers.
We'd donned insincerity as our posture groveled.
Caricatures pretended to communicate.
Hope, once ripe –
perishes as it spoils under parching sun.

Now the alphabet has shrunk to a final letter.
Not even a syllable remains.
Not unless benevolence triumphs.
Not unless life becomes edged with stones
that we believe are diamonds.

Motion for Discovery

Your Honor, if it pleases the court,
look into my eyes.
Exactly as you see me now, I ask –
Do you witness my romance?
My plea – I give my testimony –
I swear to tell you what's in my heart.
I've loved you since the moment I saw you.
I am competent to share my life with you.
I know and shall live
in accordance with our longing.
I'll never waver from my desire for you.
Please listen closely to my words.
It is my believe that our portion of time
is living inside one another's longing.
You are the cherished sparkle visible to me.
Just as bumblebees swarm
when we pass by hollyhocks,
we comprehend.
Orchards of blossoms flavor the airways –
we inhale fragrant treasure.
Clouds place us down on earth
so that we might touch poetry.
Rhymes slid over the orb of a rainbow.
Your ruling is a precious phrase of star glitter.
You scrutinize the garden of evidence.
Great willow branches reach through eons
and take up residency in my heart.
We elevate the law of verse.
Our souls will be filled
with that beloved message.
I'm awaiting your ruling.
I hope to be found innocent.
Or at least not guilty.

Flawed

Our empathy wasn't flawed.
We stretched our arms to reach destiny.
Dreams overflowed –
and took the place of questions.
Were we too quickly captives?
We became hostages wearing similar headgear.
We thought our address might be
the one between home and heaven.
But it remained empty –
happiness had been evacuated.
Chaos rushed like a flurry
of hatred being detonated.
We had been cornered
as sunshine slid away from our horizon.
With ambiguity we soldiered on.
Those Angels you spoke of hadn't vanished.
We knew passion would never trade itself
for mechanical love.
Explosive days isolated us.
Once mesmerizing smiles became grins.
We wouldn't trade places
with anyone else in the world.
There was no dialogue –
only the taunting of strangers.
Tormenting jokes were being played
on anyone diverse.
They wanted to trade rigid deities of glamour
for innocent souls.
The epilogue became a storm.
Cobalt blue night settled us – but not for long.
Blazing red blinking lights overtook us.
We must turn over the days of prejudice.
Of course we knew that we'd forever
be available to one another.
And we'd look out for our companions.
Flawed days are far too costly.

Winter's Swanish Lovesong

Who would listen
if she sang harsh and lonely melodies?
Our ears have shut down until joy is sung.
We've listened in on *goodbye love*.
We've eavesdropped on sad parting utterances.
Forced debate,
and grievous arguments leaves us cold.
Frozen like Winter's disharmony, we wept.
We wish only to bring on the bliss
before life crumples us to the ground.
We wished to shut down
the ugly pronunciations of intolerance –
we wish to find shelter.
Women aren't meant for destruction.
We create life itself.
We should allow existence to describe us.
We fuel continuance of humanity.
We aren't tokens,
and there isn't an estimate on us.
Don't warm our heart while shutting down love.
Bragging rights are tacky
when yearning is up for grabs.
Women don't need to stand in line.
We can find someone to cherish us.
We can locate someone to fund our acceptability.
Our strength is monumental.
We'd viewed suffering
while crawling from gulches.
We can assert our love
as we encourage commitment.
We can stand on the cuticle of a lake together or
hide our invisible pain.
We can march;
we can lift our wings and soar to equality.
We are lyrics coming away
from the shadows and the smoke.

We sing and never allow frost to douse our fire.
Air chills are turned away by a warming embrace.
As we progresses, joy clings to our soul.
We are Winter Swans with love-song lips.

Part Four
Sisterhood

	Page
Sisterhood Intensified	82
War Cloud Words	84
Harlots and Tramps	86
Muddled Trail	87
Our Own Landmarks	89
Looking Back for Zebras	90
My Sparkle	91
Playground Solvency	92
Another Verse	94
Goddess Needed: Inquire Within	95
Pantry	97
Co-Hosts	99
That's A Wrap	100
Smack Dab in the Center	101
Shifting Times	102

Sisterhood Intensifying

Then:
We knew that sisterhood should be intensified.
If we were to survive the mangling hold
of prejudice and hatred,
we would be required to fight oppression and win.
Lodged speeches beckoned their release.
Weighted down were our liberties.
Anger was fetched
so that we would gather together.
Slogans edged their way onto our pages.
Spurts of well-kneaded sisterhood lunged.
We'd tired of shrugging uselessly.
We'd been stranded in history by inequity.
Timidity was finally depleted.
No more slouching groans would be allows.
We readied our recital.
Singing our anthem out loud felt good.
Marching was a luster-crested event.
But there was always the bit of crisis.
We weren't the flippant *girls* they'd imagined.
Dignity decorated our faces.
We put our case on the line -
hoisting high placards naming our discontent.
If we were fired from our livelihood –
so be it.
If we were disengaged from our families –
so be it.
Darkness was no longer constructing our souls.
Our podium was built on four-post dreams.
We could dash, hurtle, crisscross,
and ignore threats.
And finally we could achieve our rights.

Now:
Ambitions slide our objectives toward the goals.
Achievement seems again to catapult

as we challenge.
We've come that proverbial long way, baby.
As a nation many inequities remain.
As a world –
the value and worth of women,
the pride of Sapphics,
must be recognized.
Lines are blurred, but vision will not fade.
The grounds beneath us are constantly shifting.
We open our arms to encircle one another.
A tide of women –
we are in a parade of courage –
and we vow to continue.
As we must.
Promises to ourselves and for our sisters
require that of us.
It is imperative.
Sisterhood intensifying?
Until?
We'll know when it is no longer required.

War Cloud Words

Words, no louder than a wasp emits, are sighed.
Vividly detailed hatred shouted its message.
Each nation's declaration was galvanized
with stealthy resolve.
When trepidation converted to fear –
terror became a shivering announcement.
There was no way back.
Such a small deed was required – barely a blemish.
Watchdogs suffered from the violent feeding frenzy.
A veiled cradle had been leavened into time's mud.
Metal twisted stick-figures were uncoiled trinkets.
Barely identifiable,
they anonymously cascaded to earth.
Hollowed-out lands, homes, and people
were estranged from their mission of life.
Death remnants left pungent air,
and hovering souls were reinvented.
Exalted, vile, and evil laughter claimed sad victory.
A desolate calendar continued digging earth.
Naked flames from a once bright ceremony
duplicated blisters of excruciating agony.
Life was haunted by inhumanity.
In a cobwebbed corner we gathered.
Delusion invaded destiny.
Rushing away was the fake charisma
of a well-armed circus barker.
No less than peace, war must be managed,
the general said.
All songs smashed into their own
silent stone of anguish.
No one had truly conquered
the darkest day ever created.
War exploded – while love imploded.
Emotions were folded between creases of flesh.
Drills scratched the glove
to find the depth of blood.

Hate's taste had forever fouled the air.
Yet perfumed trails of love curled toward heaven.
If we pressed our lips toward kindness,
would unkindness not hide?
Such a searing microcosm
had ushered in disruption.
The clasp of humanity could be assured
by an edict of compassion.
Peace with simplicity
and the majesty of perfect care
could allow each earthling a chance.
Yet villainy intruded with deliberate intent
to carve away that very decency.
Hostilities, so chaotic and cruel,
seemed every-present.
So honorable was trust and benign hearts.
Prayers were hoisted upward –
sent for heaven's charity.
The utterance fled to the open skies
of a shaded universe.
Innocence often falls away –
and is smashed as it drops.
And war cloud words were
shrieking even louder.
At least until the world
became weary of listening.
And then without contrition,
without pseudo-justice,
yet with the compassion for victim,
and not villain –
reason lived.
The sky cleared.

Harlots and Tramps

We chased down the lonely trails
of our nightmares.
They were tagging us
with the names *harlots* and *tramps*.
Slurs were spit in our direction.
Those wild women –
those youth's on Sapphic ovary hunts – were us.
We're accused of pursuit –
both scalding hot and freezing cold.
Our heads sink like furious mastiffs.
Vermillion rage assaulted our intangible desire.
We are rambunctious and we brazen it out.
Bring on the menacing slurs and cruel jokes.
Bigots seldom knock us to the ground.
We ignore most sleazy treatment.
With antiquity's credentials, I cringe.
I would be in the confines of the category below:
Lady-lover, dyke, Lesbian, and Sapphic.
I'm aware of the true harlots and tramps.
It ain't me, pal.

Muddled Trail

As I stormed the muddled trails –
my steps plunged toward adventure.
Our collective lesbian umbilical cord
was snipped.
That withering rope no longer grasped us.
Life had not chained us
to a perpetual mound of flesh.
We were released –
the twine slackened –
and we breathed on our own.
We are born of the gunk and goo
that spurts us all into the world.
Although we were nearly vacant brawn,
we escaped onto our stage.
It was our first breakout.
The next wall we went over was more difficult.
It was finding that we were not accepted.
Like-minded – sisters saved us.
We were family –
and we were one another's wild escapades.
'Good tidings' tell us we've been muddled.
So be it.
Many have followed –
and many I have pursued.
Those glorious sixties
began in horrific heavens.
All were against us –
except us.
We vocally listed infringements and infractions.
The seventies were breakout years.
We marched, we chanted,
and we tried not to hide.
Many times we were forced to run for cover.
Cover was our friends.
The eighties produced more advancement
for our cause.

We sang an accoutrement of belief.
There was a collocation exhibited
across the nineties.
Things were being done,
accomplished, and replicated.
The next decades were excursions
across our possibility.
Same-sex marriage –
damn straight.
Well, not straight.
And okay, so the future is intrigue.
Built always on yesterday,
more trails will be blazed.
Welcome to the league of sisterhood.
Antiquity has been a blast.
Our trail is only muddled
if we accept the abuse.
We are only muddled
if we conceal the genuine us.
There is nothing muddled about love.
Please don't allow anyone to ever tell you that.

Our Own Landmarks

Ridicule –
that's what they bombarded us with.
Women marching – Sapphics parading –
we were weekend warriors.
Pilgrims of our pride, sure.
Flower children replete
with playbills demanding equality –
indeed.
We were connoisseurs of justice.
Handed-down hatred often traveled incognito.
Treachery is callous; it is cowardly.
Those who would incarcerate us,
institutionalize us, and shun us –
believed themselves to be superior.
Vulnerable – we elevated our banners.
Our voices screamed.
Yet, some proverbs explained the universe
in a one-line whisper.
Created equal.
We would like our rights.
We would like our megaphone on high volume.
We're in need of landmarks.
For we have very few –
unless you count the rainbow flags.
And we are without events -
perhaps with exception of Stonewall.
I'd rather the next generation be unafraid.

Looking Back for Zebras

Pounding hooves reverberate.
A stampede follows closely behind.
I'm a shepherdess being chased.
I glance back over the shoulder
of my aged tunic.
Crossing the sinister intersection,
I locate questionable signage.
With unflappable ecstasy, I turn the corner.
Yes, I was a duck-and-cover kid,
so fear sets solidly in the midst of wonderment.
I was being stalked by society.
Lavender glossaries offered sanctuary
against the weathered steel of hatred.
If I'm not careful, I might end up demolished.
Once bent,
all accidents might conform to my armor.
Mixed with failure, and
mingled with checkerboard terror,
I reroute.
Pliant, yielding surveys offer an intermission.
Escaping rebels splash me with corruption.
Fragments of gyrating scribbles
interrupt my sad cries.
Is the sin of omission a heterosexual modifier?
I interpret a paralyzing dream, frame by frame.
When I awake, I gasp for air.
Then, crawling from a rumpled bed,
I remember.
Someone in line
at the grocery store had commented
on a weekly newspaper edition.
The woman perused the headlines.
Ellen and her wife stood proudly.
The woman blurted, "Lesbians should be killed."
Rubbing my eyes,
I knew why I'd been looking back for Zebras.
Bigots often camouflage their intent
by wearing Zebra costumes.

My Sparkle

You are my sparkle –
we live inside a wave length.
Light is manipulated –
you are my luster.
The invisibility of bleeps and bells
means nothing.
For we cling to the thickly tufted flesh of poetry.
We slide over the clouds of an orchestra.
And hide within the canvas of a rainbow's orb.
We tumbled into the core
of one another's existence.
Our love is poured
from an exquisite decanter of chance.
Each tier of eloquence evolves skillfully.
Our spirits are unpacked –
and we are highlighted.
You brighten my world.
You sing echoes of eternity into my ears.
I am safe within the touch of you.
The spark of you challenges my best.

Playground Solvency

Who knows why I fell in love with her.
She penetrated life's pitfalls and my carnal soul.
She demolished those rusted-away investments.
Exploitations were premeditated, and impulsive.
She was filled with glossed dreams.
Until they were confiscated,
she vowed to share them.
Her contour of happiness was
chomped around the edges.
Particles of earth's atmosphere had arranged us.
Every footstep nibbled away at a global carpet.
She took me with her –
on the playground.
Travel astounded us.
There was a loop –
she skirmished with it.
When I noticed she was caught in a web,
I assisted her to maneuver her way to freedom.
There were streams we waded across.
Surrounding clouds above
banked against jutting peaks.
I pointed out the open sky,
and the sunshine's ebullience.
Buoyantly, jubilantly,
she played beneath the brightness.
The storm aimed at her,
yet she never noticed.
With a jaunty exhalation,
she continued on.
We finally saw the rim
of a vast and obstinate ocean.
I wondered if she could survive.
Sluggishly drifting waves
had spewed foamy puffs.
The shoreline became filthy.
Great walls of water intruded,

and then folded back to the sea.
As if bowing with great etiquette,
fluid collapsed.
She sang in tune with the roar.
Programmed by posterity,
earth's ripening continued.
It was a constant baptism.
One portion emptied to fill another.
Plates of earth vented, vapor melted,
and illumination faded.
She viewed new designs
with luscious chasms.
Metamorphosing, yes.
Great canyons, cliffs, and mountains
postured against the sky.
She witnessed their vanity.
She meandered through
the globe's catastrophic, petrified trails.
Ropes of infinity loosen, tighten,
drop away, and fray.
They tangled – dropping her.
She slid, whirled, and tumbled.
She fell, and then rested.
She shared her playground with me.
I'll love her until my final breath.

Another Verse

Another verse – another hidden lyric.
Beyond we hear a political voice.
Words of power slap us.
They claim to be bipartisan.
They take their shark out of the pool
when they ask for our vote.
They give ego massages
when they ask for our money.
They refuse to leave a paper trail.
Their bigotry won't show.
Hide labels, and strategize –
that's the mantra.
Counting on stupidity –
they expect us to unravel the brushstrokes.
They don't want us cracking the book's spine
to look for wisdom within.
And when intolerance rules –
we attempt to notice as little as possible;
and collapse as few times as possible.
We've filled in too many blanks.
We've bowed to too many zealous demands.
Signing pacts with their truth might ignore our love.
We barter away our rainbow
before we pick up the pen.
There are the visible parts of the cleansed rhyme.
But we only view it when we aren't confined.
Objectivity is all that can be counted on.
Throughout history we've been fooled.
They bring out another verse.
It hides beneath another lyric,
and awaits acceptance.
Please never forget to fear them.
And please always remember
to make them fear you.
Fear is toxic.
Fear is also preservation's infantry.

Goddess Needed: Inquire Within

Please resurrect those Goddesses and
get them here to help.
Exhume those marble statues –
we face a conquest.
The hunt is on – bullies are alive and well.
We need resolution of the heart.
Women need world-wide recognition.
Put us on the program schedule.
Screw the Satanist theory.
We're not the ones
on the dark side of the outlet.
We're not the savage screamers.
We don't cast aspersions and spew hatred.
We don't deny others freedom,
equality, and rights.
We aren't the enemy.
Bigots want us all – also all like-minded –
to take a shuttle ride to hell.
They must want to see others suffer.
They must enjoy our sadness.
They know how to fan the stench of smoke –
they've set enough gays and lesbians aflame.
How can that be charitable?
Marching with chants of evil –
how can trying to stop a soldier
from being buried with honors be good?
When haters reach across the table and
extend a rotted handshake – we must wonder.
They question
how can we be so imprudent as to love?
As if animosity is a slick metal
aiming for our ribcage, they exterminate us.
Our love will not go to waste –
we shall not become them.
We are as we were made,
and we are who we envision ourselves to be.

I wonder if a Goddess could help us out.
There seems to be a vacancy
that only a Goddess can fill.
Applications gratefully accepted.

Pantry

Open the pantry
and enter the space of exotic women.
We come in such a magnificent array.
We are part of a variety extraordinaire.
When I flipped back the pantry door,
I was greeted by you - my exclusive woman.
You were bedecked in wonder.
No grievance reached my lips – I wanted you.
Everyone wanted you.
We were together
and then went to separate pantries.
Love was so time-consuming.
And we were young –
on the way to wherever tender hearts roam.
Before we knew it, we were stuck in middle years.
Love remained.
As wintry years of age were approaching –
I wondered what it meant – those lost years.
Scratching off one calendar's page after another
became a lonely business.
The pause in our lives was a thief we allowed.
We had shared sensuality
with endurance, vitality, and hot skin.
We tenderly disrobed,
and it was an event of sharing
the moment and the meaning.
Mouths watered and
fireworks went off in our groin areas.
Luxury opened lacy shutters
Your touch took me with you.
When our pause began,
I felt left behind.
The cards we sent began to dwindle.
We discussed others, and our lives –
only meaningless events.
Being alone had scratched us deeply.

It was as though the pantry had been emptied.
Our hearts were left on the vacant shelf.
Then we opened the pantry doors –
one final time.
We found both of our treasuries were lonely.
We had both waited for the formalities.
The Ceremony of Pantry Unveiling was ours.

Co-Hosts

We were all co-hosts –
those decades worth of friends and me.
We met with one another's approval.
So many styles of women have been there.
We were bit players
within the universe of Sapphic romance.
We were stars only within our coterie.
We marched, of course we did.
Sometimes were felt to be understudies
with microphones.
Often we were walk-ons
with label pins and chants.
Our words were the tiny print.
We were one another's makeup artists, dressers,
and scenery changers.
And listening in depended on sound-jocks –
the boom handers,
and lighting techs.
Prompters threw lines as if they were floating lassoes.
We were
the Women's Lib and Gay/Lesbian Lib proponents.
Custodians, cleaners, chauffeurs,
and greeters distributing playbills, we were.
We wrote scripts, directed the business,
and fought for equality.
We were loving co-hosts after reviews.
We wanted applause, and names on marquees.
We received a chance at changing the world.
An opportunity at bettering our land
was all we asked.
Fan bases were meager, spotlights were dim,
and sometimes nothing worked.
Our soliloquys weren't heard.
The performance wasn't over for decades –
centuries – forever.
Co-hosts?
We loved our friends.
Forever co-hosts.

That's A Wrap

Where did all the rainbows go?
Intentions are vital.
We replayed caresses.
Kisses were renewed.
Love's mighty majesty was shared.
There were invasions of hurt.
A smile is a fine diplomat.
We wouldn't allow time to corrupt us.
I dreamed of women's love.
I reedited moments that browbeat.
Gold shimmered with promise.
Hearts get tossed out.
They end up in a lost and found department.
Pleasure often belonged elsewhere.
We sometimes forgot the thunder.
We sometimes overlooked the storms.
Yet we never stopped wondering
about where the rainbows might be.

Smack Dab in the Center

Smack dab in the center of a relationship –
we were.
Reckless – for I'd barely located my tribe.
I'd just embarked on the trip to where I belonged.
I'd walked the world's loneliest streets.
I'd found my glorious woman.
With a first embrace, my soul was consecrated.
Lush and irresistible love anointed me.
In my apprenticeship, I'd faltered.
I hadn't stayed in my own lane - our lane.
A fortress filled with portraits
from the past remained.
We'd cherished one another.
She lent her lips and gave me her engaging grin.
When it came to *orgasm of the year* titles –
she aimed for a Guinness World Record.
Free-fall excitement wasn't dangerous.
We were lifetime contenders.
Ethos was a mix that made us both vulnerable.
Parental discretion was advised.
The gate of age was launched,
and our yearnings for one another continued.
I remain smack dab in the center of her.

Shifting Times

It had been years
since I'd thumbed through old, yellowed letters.
Long ago, I impatiently awaited those missives.
We were simultaneously at life's lowest point.
There was a sting of failure –
and we were human contraband.
We were robbed of our own cultures.
Understanding is mandatory.
Discordant forgiveness leaves us skeptical.
Our logic shifts tempo
and surges toward our last best effort.
Centuries detached us.
There were qualms.
Fortune's collision weakened our will to search.
Embellished pages impaired us.
Digging out was a Herculean feat.
Words became chosen weapons
that left us destitute.
Our own world of autonomy was idle.
Hopes were crimped; determination recast.
Emblems were scant – fading into oblivion.
We couldn't find one another.
Your footprints were seen leaving my side.
Through trends of darkness –
we had wandered away.
We are now allowed to live, to marry,
to be together.
The shift of time validated us.
We would no longer be incomplete.
We were never disbarred from one another.

Kieran York

Part Five

Our Path Is Time

	Page
Our Path Is Time	106
Disguised Seasons	107
Poetry Playground	108
Timely Appreciation	110
Heart Psychology	111
Internet Romance	113
Victimology of Romance	115
The Charm of Safe Harbor	116
One Version	117
Directions	118
Mist Above the Rockies	119
Earth Artist	120
Broken Us	123
Hideaway Harmony	125
The Constellation of Specimens	126

Our Path Is Time

Our path is time – the time of us.
Ink bleeds from my seasoned pen.
I see into my own exactitude.
I've shown you my x-ray.
There's my beating heart
with a hammer's pounding taps.
And there are my breathing lungs
that powerful gusts are wearing away.
My bone scans are skeletal road maps.
MRIs expose it all – my all.
From flushing blood through vessels
to witnessing a resting brain,
I am a specimen.
Words once rushed, now they seem delayed.
My sapphire ink is lingering.
Sentences that once rapidly congealed,
now form slowly.
Will bandages calm my fading ink?
Will medication improve my prose?
Will a splint mend my poetry?
Manuscript paper fills –
and my heart presses out each letter.
Moments shiver as I attempt to capture them.
I carry on – walking our path of time.

Disguised Seasons

Time needs examining –
for hidden evidence.
It may be harboring disguised seasons.
There are barren, desolate links of eternity
that often curdle before they've been used.
There are days that should be superimposed
across each framed and fortuned reminiscence.
The daybreak
of each season materializes secretly.
Disassembling forecasts and formulas,
we search for what's ahead of us.
Our eyes can't always focus
so far ahead of existence.
Night's coolness hauls us
into morning's arms.
We are captivated
by those intoxicating yesterdays.
We are propelled
toward the endlessness of tomorrow.
Summer thrusts its designer luminescence
across each of our horizons.
Autumn sometimes begins
with fiery temperatures,
and ends with the trickery of icicles.
Winter often issues manacles,
shackling us to frozen intervals.
Finally Spring unlocks the chains.
All those colors drop in on us
as though they are visitors from long ago.
All sunshine gives an adrenalin rush.
We've been kissed by the Muses,
Goddesses, Angels – and Sweethearts.
The entire celestial hierarchy became our guest.
Each season warbles its own whimsical anthem.
Lyrics seep into one another as time is used.
We awaken in our own season – each morning.
It is too glorious not to highly recommend.

Poetry Playground

Guitar music formed gleaming acoustics.
Seated, the three sat slouched in a circle of radiance.
The Poetry Playground Group commenced rituals.
Password: Inspiration.
The atmosphere was transient - a gentle breeze sighed.
The nest of poets harvested their dreams.
Seekers – they were on an odyssey of vibrant phrases.
Gauzy, winged lyrics soothed.
Exhilaration was becoming vision.

Exalted Pleasure: What is the earth's oldest color?
Hushed Melancholy: It's the same hue as night.
Exalted Pleasure: I think it is *sunshine* color.
Prophesy Guardian: I agree sunshine might be the color.
(The trio of poet-giggles are blown across the playground)
Exalted Pleasure: Or perhaps rainbow is the color.
Hushed Melancholy: I don't believe *rainbow* is a color.
Exalted Pleasure: I insist it must be a color – rainbow.
Hushed Melancholy: No, that's an arrangement of different shades.
Prophesy Guardian: Shades are indeed colors.
(Searching their laptops, the three poets sighed)
Hushed Melancholy: I can't find anything to solve the problem.
Exalted Pleasure: I vote that rainbow is the most ancient color.
Hushed Melancholy: I stick by the darkness answer.
Exalted Pleasure: Night is darkness – a force of nature.
Prophesy Guardian: Often a pleasurable time of dreams.
Hushed Melancholy: Well daylight is only a mood.
Exalted Pleasure: So it must be a rainbow.
Prophesy Guardian: Rainbows are a combination – inclusive.
Hushed Melancholy: That's a silly concept.
Exalted Pleasure: My motto is – if it lacks humor – it's useless.

Hushed Melancholy: I concede rainbows *are* enjoyed as
they glow.
Exalted Pleasure: Then the 'first color' mystery is solved
 – rainbow!
Prophesy Guardian: Yes, meeting adjourned.
Love and laughter can begin.

The music perked up as a rainbow illuminated the sky.
The poets believed it was resting atop the mountains.
The next gathering of The Poetry Playground Group
would explore the feasibility of a mountain wearing a
rainbow.

Timely Appreciation

We are convinced time is both benefactor
and bandit.
We count on the benevolence of our earth.
Moments rally as they fracture - then tick away.
As parceled out, they are earth's degrees.
As lived,
a litany of events becomes reminiscent charm.
Increments are varied with pastoral backdrops.
Oceans beat time by waving laps toward shore.
But who is Mother Nature?
She crouches behind the shoulders of cliffs.
She wades into waters with depth beyond light.
Living those imposing, elite days,
she is accompanied by time.
She rushes so quickly, she is barely recognizable.
She orchestrates a contradictory world.
Our respite is searched.
Vintage years are dotted with asterisks.
Lurking catastrophes produce unsettling visages.
They wedge between rich-textured wonder, and us.
She knows how rebellious it can be.
Within the epochs of our tired centuries
are vendors of energy.
The dichotomy of all is that souls are rearranged.
Terrain, events, and fortune –
they impact us with each clench of the fist,
and each smile of a sunset.
She presses near our pragmatic souls.
And teaches her lesson.
Time takes us to our place.

Heart Psychology

If psychology is the meaning of our narrative –
I'm lost within my own joke.
Searching problems has never enlightened me.
Hunting out the disillusion of defeats and decline
only confuses me.
Peek-a-boo guesses, I named the procedure.
That was after a friend
had gone through three therapists.
Each of them had differing conclusions.
The diagnosis ranged in opinions and prescriptions.
I suggested that life might be too precious
for the theory of guesswork.
My friend looked sadly into my eyes and
muttered her way
through five more broken relationships.

But therapy sessions offered her company.
She was analyzing the docs.
Handing out good marks
for good performances.
Our laughter coalesced.
When giggles faded, she frowned.
She asked what if she found a wise woman.
Don't look at me, I chided.
She promptly told me she *wasn't*.
We laughed again.
Louder this time.
She shrugged and told me
that it was a way of circulating her money.
That laugh was all that kept her alive.

Then one day she was rescued
by a very wise woman.
Together, they moved to Ohio and
happily spent over two decades together –
and many more to come.

Every holiday greeting card that I've received
from the couple includes humor.
Some years were about Snoopy and the snowman.
I hid the ones showing Santa's nudity.
One year had to do with the bodily functions
of reindeer.
Last year Maxine graced the card.
Valentine's Day must offer
a special psychological breakthrough.
The cards sent
have never included clothed cupids.

Internet Romance

Toss the dice.
Guides, tutors, educators, magicians -
they present a path.
Although trivial, although mundane –
a message awaits.
Arms stretch to explore
the heightened emotional reaction.
Each key means a command performance.
Prompts become comical events.
Words, images, and noise
oozes from the keyboard.
Where is the disruptive behavior?
Wait a moment or two.
The Net ticks along smoothly –
we are to believe.
Precious passion flowers grow
within my computer.
Smoking hot villains might await us.
Where is the delete button?
All solutions are on one key or another.
Hairline cracks on the screen are repaired.
We create our own amped up victory.
The place between previous and next
is where we snuggle.
Soon we are incoherent lap dogs.
Friends surround us.
Others shout, and a hoarse whisper
comes from the corner.
Transmitting words
are electronic surveillance tapes.
Deflected are recriminations,
ignominiously challenging.
Arrogance is randomly offered.
Ingredients range from juvenile, myopic,
and conspiratorial to –
intelligent, warm, humorous, and vital.

We file our emotions, and then recite our hearts.
If contemptuous breaches are savage, we escape.
Or we are reeled in beside the catch of the day –
all *duped* up?
Romance, with the cyber-enchantress,
can offer tripwire deception,
or pure untainted love.
I clicked the menu titled *Heart*.
The agenda is hidden.
There might be lovely women waiting.
Tenderness is their offering.
Chancy – all of life is a dice toss.

Victimology of Romance

Maudlin tears of tragedy flowed.
We've all be the perpetrator.
We've all be the victim.
Admission makes us human.
The low purr of shame ignites –
then flickers to the 'off' position.
Apologies lounge with our hearts
before they finally disintegrate.
We've disappointed
and we've been disappointed.
Shock waves electrocuted us - slightly.
Our tangled routine started over.
We would never hurt one another again.
We were in the state of revision.
More tolerant; more considerate –
we would be.
All the missing particles would congeal
with our souls.
Yet, we had added our own footnotes.
They were addendums with dents and abrasions.
We knew they were there –
we signed the formal requests – regardless.
Hand in hand, we crossed the secret grimness.
Curtains were pulled and
unhappiness was ushered in.
When love is amputated by cruelty –
it can never be salvaged again.
Unpacking one's interior requires trust.
When love is plied from our hearts –
we have no way of locating one another – ever.

The Charm of Safe Harbor

Anxiety attempts to lean as far forward,
toward us, as possible.
Our decisions are secure.
Relished lovers or lascivious acquaintances –
romance comes in different cartons.
If it's flimsy,
we wash down hurt with self-deception.
We unpack our dreams and become ourselves.
Laughter, sun, rain, day or night – we accept.
An artist invents a landscape.
There is a watercolor gala.
The wash of prismatic paint comforts us.
A chill slaps us when we awaken alone.
A world filled with an infusion of fun
is our inheritance.
Optimism's sheen appears on a sweet corner.
If we trip, we stand again.
Endless sunsets become our classroom windows.
Remembrances –
like battered wings made new –
embrace us.
We are meant for our planet's security wrap.
We distance ourselves from episodes of harshness.
Our knapsacks are filled with poems
that are poured across the shore of optimism.
Docking are the ships of precious memories.
Waves had surfaced with soothing visibility.
High voltage affairs become pure enchantment.
When we find the security of complete love –
we must learn its name.
Mine is called the charm of safe harbor.

One Version

History rarely deals from a clean deck.
Our Sapphic past zigzags.
We attempt to extrapolate truth
from instant replays.
Our lives scatter like sparkling sound bites.
Ideas imprint our minds with possibility.
Lesbians are a version – sometimes hidden.
Sometimes shunned,
along with our meanings – we sob.
Sometimes overlooked,
along with our desire – we laugh.
Love has been sacrificed.
A great crashing over-voice is prejudice.
Our song is drowned by strength.
Is it that we believe in the power of goodness?
We reach for that strand of light
that births friendship.
We belong together.
We measure our course by relative motion.
Bravery props us up.
Life is not only an unavoidable delay –
it is our gift.
Our landscape is written, spoken and handed down.
Our geography is forgotten
like the preciously placed faces of yesterday –
the ones lost to us forever.
Certainly during history
we have been tactically eradicated.
We must climb higher
for new thoughts and strategies.
If not, we shall only continue to disappear
behind the horizon of our legacy.
I give up only one version of me.

Directions

If I had directions,
I would take life on the road.
I'd parcel out the world's great land.
Each glorious acre
would be a peace-required zone.
Peace.
A garden of summer flavors would be birds,
butterflies, flowers, terracotta and sunshine.
If there were no hostilities,
consider the prosperity.
This lifetime does not always show me
that wondrous moment.
It will take so many steps –
and so many eons.
Hands of a clock reach for me.
My words encourage hope for new generations.
If each heart is pursued by kindness,
it could happen.
And if our direction is never located –
we all have failed.
I wish I could issue a free pass to goodness.
There would be no greed, no hatred, and no envy.
The directions would be
to embrace consideration.
Directions to Peace.
Why not?
We should first learn the anatomy of a grin.

Mist Above the Rockies

Mist has lifted
just enough to glide over the foothills.
Near earth's surface, fog gathers.
As the mystical air circulates,
there is a swirl of mingling clouds.
I don't reside on an impersonal planet.
Barbed-wire suggests guidelines –
and enclosures.
My hangout is here.
Even steady rocks eventually crumble.
Streaming waters, sharp storms,
and buckling strips
of optimism rearrange each path.
In one way or another –
it can all be evaporative – yet productive.
So quietly so, and with such fragility,
that I can barely hear it.
I believe in the earth's open arms,
and the sky's floating message.
We find our way through the mist,
toward where we belong –
where sunshine polishes our smiles.

Earth Artist

Earth is awhirl within the sprawling heavens.
It is designed as our natural inheritance –
of that I am certain.
A potter's hands sculpt earth.
Those hands reshape clay,
and interpret precious clumps of soil.
Those hands cut clay blocks with wire strings.
There is the lift and plunge
of a fist into a rotating globe.
Guesswork begins,
and it turns into the calculating touch of skill.
Earth's direction began unpredictably
as it unleashed across this universe.
In throwing clay, with each whirl of the wheel,
creation is forged.
Spinning disks promise a free ride
to imagination.
Circular, orbital, as with the galaxies,
the wheel rotates.
Knobs of gray, tan, red –
and in between colors of wonder
stitch expression into reality.
The cool, damp clay is adroitly formed
by wet hands that allow the wheel to dictate its pull.
Edging clay upward is a communication –
a directive between inspiration and touch.
A container is born, a sculpture is invented.
Clay grows tall,
edging as the sediment-sweetened sponge drips.
Stoneware is formed.
The land's face connects, for it is tilled.
Molding, the potter caresses.
Framing the terrain's bounty into contours
of beauty produces life's bounty.
Fine ceramics are engineered
as they are cradled by knowing touches.

Lessons of clay reflect chance,
just as our globe's destiny presents itself.
The crust fades when fragile material is stressed.
The clay is place aside and restored by time.
Time settles both terracotta and territory.
Time strengthens both
and gives each endurance.
With insured plasticity – art is constructed,
and becomes pliable, and then resilient.
It is sturdier than raw clay.
Learning patience with each effort,
the potter comes to know life's wait.
Drying time produces its own lesson.
As the vessels and creations await firing,
the artist accepts the timing of existence.
Drying time is where patience seems most at home.
When the leather-hardened art is fired,
fortune takes command.
Cone-monitored temperatures assist
in predicting creation.
Speculation is only a dream that presents a lesson.
For preparation corrects mistakes;
and prevents mistakes.
The beauty of earth
takes on another form of loveliness.
From the kiln comes bisque.
After it is dipped into vats of glaze,
brushed with oxide, and twirled,
it becomes an artist's vortex.
Chemistry has mingled the best rainbow designs
from inside a potter's mind.
Sunrise colors and twilight hues
blend into nature's visionary promise.
Although there is an awareness
buried somewhere within,
there seems to be no way
to truly encroach upon reality.
There is only imitating nature.

Nothing is overlooked, and nothing is ignored.
Inspiration finds its reverence
and appreciation of life's components.
Expressing, translating, and conducting impulses,
energy flows from hands that touch earth.
Connecting, yielding, and sheltering,
are part of the process.
There is the beguiling swirl of invention and vision
when indentations are created from a serrated tool.
The corner of the art's nucleus must be shown.
From the glow of a prism, to the textures of life,
it becomes a replicated knowing of the universe.
Earth is often scarred, punctured, and battered.
Yet with peace, patience, and acceptance,
there is love's reprisal.
It is captured within a magnificent reward called art.
Earth's alloys and bonding agents
are nearly as complicated
as life's earthlings.
In each unfurling of creativity's wisdom
a miracle is formed.
An earth artist's task is to sculpt
an offering of pleasure, and meaning,
and most importantly,
to include the texture of love.

Broken Us

Wadded up and thrown away was our love.
Romance rushed from us without calling back
- as I'd imagined.
It became quick-frozen – hard as solid granite.
Silly life – all twisted and congested
– had once cherished us.
Aspirations rolled from corner to cliff.
From wrapped arms warming
to the chill of ice – we traveled away.
We'd tumbled beneath dissimilar dreams.
Grabbing, you'd reached in
and your fist tore my heart from its home.
It had been securely placed –
tucked within my ribcage.
Although I'd lent it out to you.
Broken we were.
Tattered disarray is where I reside alone.
That happens when souls
can't do without one another?
I hear the beats wrapping –
but it's only simulation.
The vacant place within my breast remains.
And it will forever subside near my desire.
If you aren't at my side –
I want no other ally.
If I don't have your love,
my rumpled soul will remain
where touch levitates
and becomes the cast of yesterday.
I'll be isolated, severed from all sensuality
throughout my tomorrows.
My devotion will remain as I stay behind.
What should have been – wasn't.
Love can never be annihilated,
however it is disheveled – distorted.
Sometimes I pretend the vessel of togetherness

is again filled.
Yet when I check closely, I see it has vanished.
I wonder if my love for you is healing
so that we might be repaired.
With spindly hope – I'll wait for you.
As you said, two people in love can never let go.
Isn't 'reconvene' only a formal farewell?
I'm sorry that we were partners in breaking us.

Hideaway Harmony

Hideaway harmony –
we awkwardly cherish one another.
We rotate toward love's clinging bond.
Enlightened, we know our involvement.
Commitment begins with a question.
We both know the answer before words are spoken.
With careful introspection we observe passion.
We once were pale and neutral.
It was a complex and classic admiration.
Surrender means taking another look.
Your classroom was a class act.
Discs of music whirl.
As if crates of combustibles pivot around us,
a muscular shift of the universe happens.
You dispatch great quantities of eye jewelry.
Wink away, gorgeous.
We were in the middle of belief.
The sky's gold was significant.
You threw a kiss to the moon.
Corners of our brain stayed brave.
We finally realize day's transparency.
You are a part of my life's most blessed night.
Your arms are a hospitable wrap.
We hadn't told one another.
Words hid beneath symbolism.
When we brush up against one another –
we are certain.
We are cherished.
It was our hideaway harmony that entices us.

A Constellation of Specimens

I
Our nerve-endings bleeped when we met.
Your interview made me think in slow motion.
I didn't understand the well-hugged hypothesis.
I tolerated the gift of you.
How could I know that I was exploring the
flowering of our romance?
I thought years must be accumulated
before love happened.
Resources needed to be searched out.
There was confinement in my dreams.
We sliced away at impasses.
Compensation required more than infrequent guests.
We side-stepped our own mandates.
Of course impressions were inadequate.
Designated love had alleged forever.
Self-indulgence reverberated sounds of our decision.
The journey consumed us.
Needing a diagnosis, we feebly flexed.
We etched out our laurels across the globe.
Is this how falling in love feels?

II
We scrutinized the vista of romance.
My eyes were moist – we were unifying.
No doubt about it – I savored happiness.
There was laughter
even when our affair seemed to stall.
The joy never evacuated us – we eventually thawed.
Exploring the universe of women – we were taunted.
I shivered when your glib voice teased me.
What a massive quantity of loveliness you are.
I never protested being your accomplice.
We never once forfeited hope.
Yes we stalled and were immobilized.
Yet even our blustering words authenticated us.

We chased away the conical torches.
You declared yourself; I disclosed myself.
We enhanced all that we'd promised.

III
Echoes became fragments as ashes smoldered.
Years attempted to severe and erase all that sealed us.
A stony, coiled fence encircled us – protected us.
We never vacated all that we coveted.
Missing particles were immune to intrigue.
We were above touch and beneath reach.
Our affair digested every litany.
Doubt slid across us – we couldn't evict love.
We'd have none of it – we lamented.
Because we tried so hard to eliminate schisms,
we learned the art of by-passing conflict.
We refused to be sabotaged.
Even when we jousted, we ignored turmoil.
Dormancy never was ours.
Static, sickly silence never overtook us.
Allegiance to one another never tarnished.
Our explanation of love was never gutted.
We hung in there and invented our own bluffs.
Protests were articulated, catalogued,
and forgotten.
You remained; I stayed.
We were.

IV
We became sprinkles on one another's flesh.
We were jewelry enhancing one another's flash.
I have always been indebted to your bling.
You've been grateful for my role as joker.
Romance was never ignored.
No mystique ruined our assignments.
Whenever and wherever desire invited –
we were there with smiles.
Love song chased away vitriolic days.

Our achievements circumvented banality.
There was so much we never understood –
or allowed one another to understand.
If love makes life feel good –
well, isn't that the point of it all?
Our agenda is to recall those excellent times.
And to construct more.
Memories bring out all other sides.
Together – we are one another's moments.
For we are a constellation of specimens.

Kieran York

Part Six
Muse Of The Meadow

	Page
Muse of the Meadow	132
Conversing With the Muse	135
A Litany of Ecstasy	136
Benevolent	137
Invisible Folly	138
Dance of the Wind-Swept Lilacs	140
Revisiting	141
Please Warn Me	142
Mortal Kisses	144
Relationship	145
Austerity Measured	146
Meadows & Memories	147
Creators and Cathedrals	148
Library	150
My Raconteur	152

Muse of the Meadow

I
There was a passion and there was a dignity.
Emotions are difficult to blend
when it comes to human qualities.
Locating the center comes first.
Our Muse of the meadow hides messages.
A whisper in my ear,
told me to stay near.
And she mentioned
I shouldn't forget to bring my heart.
My Muse is always exactly where
and when I need her most.

II
My Muse is adrift in her power.
She is aware of her force.
I am aware of her force.
Each moment, each heart-song,
is there to understand
the intricate formation of my sweet Muse.
Enticement and gratitude
becomes the rustic elegance.
Symphonies extract reality.
An artist is thrust against an image.
There is courage possessed by every woman.
Creativity demands freedom of spirit.
When there is no conflict –
art becomes extinct.
Set it up, she shouts instructions.
A noble guide into illusion points out the place
where virtue has not evaporated.
With inspiration, I rush toward
my primitive, cognitive surrender.
Staged, lauded, I examine my classic cravings.
There is a pastoral rapture
as I reach across the terrestrial night.

A special valise houses me, absorbs me,
and allows me to recuperate.

III
Nature is enhanced with perfection's paradigm.
I often meld into the same genius tank –
where I once nearly suffocated.
Within the confines of passion,
my Muse overwhelms.
My soul is a visage seen by only her.
What a chaste and astute search.
Some pantomime attempts to diffuse my poetry.
Pragmatic myths cuddle me
as I plunge against the earth's hard crust.
I cling to the higher purpose of rhyme.
I am a voyager flooding an alphabet.
Prompting me is my Muse –
I've nicknamed her Honeysuckle.
She tells me not to redecorate.
That would make me an imposter.
Being counterfeited demolishes my enterprise,
she warns.
Treason only coaxes isolation.
And never, she insists,
become aglow with self-recrimination.
Or else – or *else* my spirit might find expulsion.
Words will become muzzled before the ink dries.
Take that, unworthy mortal.

IV
My angered Muse tromps me.
Unfolding pain and flaunting it
might sound concocted.
Creativity wasn't enhanced –
it skulks out another existence.
A dusty, upholstered reverie soon appears.
I became disassembled; I am unequipped.
I hunger for the mere flicker

of the precious anthem.
Solitude is sung – I serenade the challenge.
Suddenly I was jamming experience
into my backpack.
My Muse came and went –
watching my struggle.
Tantalizing memories came from the sampling
of yesterday.
I mourn my lost hours.
But in their place is tranquility.
My heart was wrung bloodless
when I dismissed my Muse.
But with her return,
I am again able to chase that regal illusion.
I'd been a witness during her vacation.
Now, my alphabet glistens with a lucid quest.
Word conjuring with a Muse is a venerable event.
Even love is much finer
when being kissed by a sweet Muse.
Ah, Honeysuckle –
she remains extraordinary enchantment!

Conversing With the Muse

Life's ceiling is designed from within, she taught.
My murky, liquid eyes understand the premise.
As if gazing into phosphorescence,
I am magnetized by her image.
Passion can never be muzzled.
Words must be refugees – even from death.
A Sage is always there.
Premonitions trick us.
Nerves traverse a path toward confusion.
Warmth binds the very luminosity that reflects me.
My energy shrieks out a postscript.
Life's contours evoke an imbued acceptance.
Grief is a bothersome obstacle.
It scatters plots.
Aspirations float above
as if they are grains of gold.
Gleaming flecks glide
as if they are petite kites.
Souls are liberated by distant lanterns.
Gates swing open as safety stalks me.
Impulses are overtaken –
orchestrated by silence.
Embossed cards express the values
of a venting scribe.
Jargon freefalls.
My Muse expresses pleasure.

A Litany of Ecstasy

Romance is a litany of ecstasy –
it is pure lace in the beginning.
Thoughts are resilient
when they turn away teardrops.
We slide into our lives,
hoping for a rainbow heirloom.
We are in coercion – nothing else will do.
Falling stars are a fascination.
Scientific documentation is pure wonder.
Interplanetary authenticity is a belief system.
But structural realism is within our grasp.
It feels more like us.
We climb twisted vine of vison
through orbital galaxies.
Unorthodox protons call out to our quest.
Scooping desire encourages us
to turn towards home.
Earth's songs are heard where meadows live.
And we are inheritors of understanding.
Opposition comes from the interior and exterior.
Vision unifies sensitivity.
Passion is our heredity, and more – our legacy.

Benevolent

The mention of her name reorders memories.
Her face is always recognizable.
We were competitive.
Our visible identities were self-inflicted.
We tried desperately to preserve our resemblances.
We tried giving only what wouldn't destroy us –
individually, and to one another.
Emotions are easily muted – sabotaged.
We blink at one another's faults.
For years we've toured, without encroaching.
Emancipation was agreed upon.
When we wept, our chants were in unison.
Dialogues followed us down the corridor
of our affair.
But destiny lived inside the music.
Retrogressive thought directed us
to reach toward love.
Songs toppled us.
We were casualties, demolished by years.
We forever cared.
We were compensated for our plans.
We declined mutual dispersal.
Although age accelerated the intricacies,
we clung to one another.
Some uneventful benevolence
found its place in us.
Humanity is love's truest requirement.

Invisible Folly

Sex is an invisible folly.
Then why do we call it silk?
And why do we refer to love as a fragile anchor?
Certainly cherishing someone is analogous
to a pedigreed, sibilant explosion.
With quickened, rushing pulses,
and molten passions –
even flirtation begins to pulverize us.
We have the propensity to imitate
a newly formed star.
We unravel –
atom by atom, by molecule, by molecular cell.
Belonging to someone is a flavor –
an additive tossed in the steaming global pot.
Securing one another requires
the ingredients be correct.
We ground ourselves into the snippets
of conversation.
We forfeit prior barricades.
With a giant's aplomb,
we reach across the space of reason.
We grasp the expansion of puffy concerns.
Everyone has the ability to escape the grasp
of a pledge.
Momentary chills might mean *beware*.
Our stoicism divests us of fear.
Monograms fade into the ebullience of retreat.
Defiance pilots us to a day of veiled mornings.
Autonomous daydreams break apart.
Absorbed in deliberation,
confusion surrounds us.
Metronome smiles generate
a bumper-sticker solution to loneliness.
We confront amenities that burst into our decision.
Submission illuminates our freedom.
We once were corseted –

now we are adrift in nudity.
We'd hoped to supplement one another.
Invisible folly, along with my heart and soul,
could never be used as collateral.
The right one will be visible.
We'll know her without question.
We shall see her – and recognize her.

Dance of the Wind-Swept Lilacs

A lilac's coloring is a mesmeric inducement.
Showy purples, luscious pinks, and tender whites –
they propagate with ease and gentle warmth.
They lift and twirl –
cordial enough for vamping at will.
Spring basks them in glory –
conceit authenticates each blossom.
They become schemers –
calculating irrepressible intimacy.
They live in the breeze's arms –
pirouetting just for laughs.
Frivolity is their best line of defense.
It is true they might be chosen
to decorate a woman's breast.
Unpretentiously –
a corsage competes for smiles.
The blooms encourage touching hands to lingering.
A cluster of purple is presented to a lover.
Coquettes, in full lavender makeup, entice.
An embracing charm produces fragrances
of memory and distinction.
Scents become coded postscripts –
with a trail of beguiling farewells.
Lilacs are all about flirtation.
They are swirling ballerinas
requesting our attention.
They long for our love –
you might say they desire us.
I offer you a morning bouquet –
to show my fondness.
Perhaps both the Lilac and I
might form a seduction.

Revisiting

Your love is my poetry.
Your laughter is my verse.
Lyrics are your glance.
And your touch is my rhyme.
Your adventure is my aspiration.
Your sense of justice is my teacher.
Your moral compass has my admiration.
Your knowledge is my library.
Your soul is my mentor.
Your adoration is a wordless sonnet.
Your trust is my justification.
Our togetherness is my belief.
Our laughter is constant, and is my happiness.
Our dancing is my joy
Thank you for lending your strength,
devotion, beauty and you.
Your faith makes me finer.
Your assurance makes me stronger.
Your words take me to where I wish to be.
I shall accompany you –
for I love that you are my courage.
You tell me you are impressed with
the silliness of my poetry.
It is something I can do for you.
Although, I think we have all that we need.
One another.

Please Warn Me

Unrestricted activities are within my sphere.
Apologies are complicated bluffs for time.
Unhappiness is a memory
that slides from my lifetime.
Bad excuses rake my heart.
Resurrected libretto is hidden behind a mask.
Currents of reality are burdens of pain.
Details smooth out our identity.
Heroes and heroines require observation.
I covet poetical kisses,
and delight in roses at twilight.
Foreshadowing our impulses,
we manufactured eroticism.
In the opinion of the entire universe,
I should have known better.
I'd believed my chronicles to have swarmed me.
The voice of reason wasn't what I needed most.
That was a given.
I'd been abandoned by a few.
Although rendered gone –
they've now returned.
The flicker of love was not depleted after all.
Betrayal was an intrusive planting of deceit.
Scammed –
it was an abusive stampede across my heart.
They say we harvest our own grim mistakes.
Misrepresentation crawled out
of a ravine of hatred.
From what I believed
to be the epicenter of happiness,
I'd been blindfolded
and led directly into a snare's grasp.
Lagging indicators of smirking emotions
stood their ground.
I thought we'd been tender stewards.
Mockery offered its own description.

Our *love* had fallen fast asleep –
yet we were wide awake.
Lampooned, and being struck by travesties,
I asked only to be warned next time.

Mortal Kisses

Love isn't all that predictable.
When it shatters, my planet is forlorn.
I've traveled through deception, cheating,
and abandonment
with minimal damage.
It's survivable.
Recuperation is perpetual.
That's all I really know about it.
I try not to count character disorders.
Or buckle up blame.
Slight of heart games are going on.
There are always mischievous DNA recipes
lounging around.
Life lulls a few untranslatable and damaged lyrics.
I glance around for gates along the swath I traipse.
Some of my memories have gone stale.
That is a huge assist to my happiness.
I need the time for immortal romance –
and smiling.

Relationship

We tumbled directly into
one another's existence.
We thumbed through each other's thoughts.
Our expressions poured
through the exquisite decanter of love.
We unpacked our spirits for –
and because, of each other.
Skillfully, each tier of eloquence evolved.
The proliferation of spirit allowed
our mutual glimpse.
Cuffed into reflection, we stacked memories.
We embroidered our best around each other.
Without glossing, we highlighted.
We were stated in real time with bona fide hearts.
Our ingredients were exchanged.
That tradeoff converted us and our meaning.
We didn't distort our relationship.
We became intrinsic perfection as
our words were recited.
What we have together means most.
Stepping into the embrace of arms opened widely –
sweet.
Hands brushing a forehead with softness –
soft.
Promises echoed *eternity* through me.
My vow presented existence to her.
It is an activated exchange –
there is more than one winner.
We mean something now.
We are a relationship.

Austerity Measured

How does austerity measure up?
Elitists flounced
and the impoverished grumbled.
The human race could use a checkup.
Have we examined our underpinnings?
Have we counted our assets?
We place repellant around –
to chase away dormancy.
Theft disrupts our trusting nature.
Gluttony makes us less astute.
Discrepancies ruin our aesthetics.
Who can solve our problems?
Politicians aren't economists.
The rulers of state use muscular words.
Second term they become canonized.
With acerbic wit,
they launch into modern nobility.
We love our rascals.
No matter what turbulence they cause.
No matter how poisonous their pretense becomes.
They'll be allowed to pinch the jazz out of us.
We'll consent to it – maybe we'll insist upon it.
We lost the measuring stick years ago.
I believe that might have been about the time
when voting began in earnest.

Meadows & Memories

Parties in the meadows and clearings are best.
They are animated, and they arouse.
They are titillating.
Vile and savage hearts soon heal.
They convert to gracious and kind.
Humiliation intervenes.
A droll humor improves.
Those seedier than a hermit are not chastised.
The mission is to entice laughter.
We giggle against one another's shoulders.
Thoughts gallop across the clearing's verdant growth.
There is a place where fondness captures our spirit.
The woodlands are on a mission.
The celebration of nascent generations is on!
Devoutly akin with the cause – the sky opens.
No one is allowed to be lost.
Who wants to be accused of unraveling a fractal?
The authority of our meadowland is intimidating.
Unpacking were knapsacks brimming with formulas.
Designs of happiness spray out in a flurry.
Influences are both meteoric, and enchanting.
The pines and spruce take on the anatomy of a cave.
The fragrances of florid wildflowers softened the edge.
The vision is of an anointed occasion.
Being there is dialing the exact complete vista.
The meadow makes me smile.

Creators and Cathedrals

When the Creator and I met –
there were no biblical whiskers and robes.
I detected no thrashing floods, hurricanes,
or earthquakes.
There were no commands –
it was left to conscience.
There were no echoes of a baritone voice
booming through a polished cloud.
Nothing resembling garbled choruses
were warbled.
The pastoral setting was wonderfully empty.
Absent were ghouls, goblins and grotesque spirits.
Acolytes guided themselves.
No charge of lightning swam the length
of my nerves.
I felt the burn of radiance within my heart.
The voyage within my mind was jovial – safe.
I had envisaged ravishing introspection.
Redemption might be difficult, I thought.
But it was 'as is' living.
It was an elliptical blink –
yet I felt it deeply.
For I was formed from me.
Mitigated were my trivial sins.
Wisdom balanced the event.
Delicate poetry was my contrition.
Spatial, tender judgments were codified missives.
I was left to be my own enigma.
Harmony was a sumptuous parting gift.
Asceticism was there and would remain.
The Creator's face was projected on my mind.
For that face lived within me.
It surrounded me
as if it was my home within the meadow.
And within the universe was my cathedral.
Within the cadence of my walk –

I heard my song.
Thought streamed
and was converted to prayer.
And I was no longer stranded.

Library

Within the stacks of academia
I located the College of Sapphic Wonder Library.
One section caught my attention –
Mosaic Hypothesis.
As I thumbed through the bookshelves,
I noticed her.
The grandiosity of eloquence was before me.
She read to me –
tutoring my quizzical expression.
Books of lacerated wisdom were excluded.
They had been provided
by the bully nations of the past.
The gaze her eyes expressed was soothing.
We knew life better since historical errors
called us names.
I wanted to kiss her lips
as they moved across her lecture.
Each synopsis confirmed our agreement.
The kinetic elements enticing our skin
were tempestuous.
Sequential waves of desire were smothering me.
I wanted her that completely.
Cosmic energies, she teased.
Had quantum mechanics realigned my deep sigh?
Each verse she read became power incarnate.
String theory was a mysterious ensemble.
Transitory intricacies
were sewn within her intonation.
The fabric of supposition,
she explained, surrounded us.
Cognitive skills challenged us.
History's visual theatrics
became edifying invitations.
My psyche needed recuperative dexterity
to keep up with her.
She rushed answers as we took an ontological voyage.

Goddess literature was only an arm reach away.
She invited me.
I could join her on the tour of empiricism.
Poetry was beckoning us.
Hand in hand,
we visited the aisles of analytical sensations.
We walked through
the ceremonial reference room.
I'd never met a more talented bibliotheca.
She whispered in my ear,
"Interlocutors are necessary for the formation
of exploratory love."
What a turbulent tour she'd taken me on.
Her wall of words uttered magic.
A longstanding affair with libraries is my delight.

My Raconteur

The best story ever was about whimsy.
I never wanted anything
to be measured in reality.
Ebullience was offered –
and she was just the one to offer it.
With a plume of comedy,
her eyebrows were raised.
No gutter snipes allowed, she insisted.
That might have been a witticism.
Her nameplate read *Loopholes*.
She speedily cranked laughter's handle.
Waving off imposters,
she told me the story of us all.
Protagonists are sublime figures of imagination.
Antagonists spout loathsome manifestos.
The emotional fuse boxes of show time sizzled.
We became adrift castaways.
Each actress was on a wisdom search.
Expletives were part of the script.
As the storyteller chattered,
stage action continued.
What a lulling narrative.
My heart unsealed,
and a grin gathered across my face.
Her sparkling repartees muffled my giggle.
Anecdotes required legends, she said.
Her curtain lowered on a self-revelatory moment.
Capsizing the drama was laughter.
I love the way life paints in patterns.
My raconteur's final speech was about us.
Existence is scrolled
in both melancholy and mirth.
She knew I was falling in love with her.

Kieran York

Part Seven

The Realm of Belonging

	Page
The Realm of Belonging	156
Nomadic Habitat	158
Torchlight Extravaganza	159
Shelter and Solace	160
Artistic Endeavor	161
Couples	162
Aphrodisiac	163
Savory Heartbeat	164
Cantilevered Over Desire	165
Fetching Delight	166
Poetic Blueprints	168
Captivating and Youthful Amaretto	169
A Singular Poet	171
A Woman Named Unremarkable	173
Unlocked Woman	175
Longing and Belonging	176

The Realm of Belonging

My lady is amazing,
and is also blazing hot.
There is such a reassured timidity
about her demeanor.
She shies away from publicity, and crowds.
I want to always be at her side.
She saves a place for me there.
She rests the tips of her fingers against my lips.
As she traces my kiss,
her eyes follow her touch.
She is tender and she is formidable.

She is my Sapphic supplier
of butterflies, roses, and sunshine.
She lifts me on wings,
enchants me with blossoms,
and brightens each corner of my day.
She gives my life flight –
and gifts me with all of her delight.
Dancing toward me,
her walk is the glide of a waltz.
Linking, our embrace is tender.
She's lured me to her.
It is what we each want –
every moment of our lives.

Throughout our lives together,
I had believed I'd pursued her.
Nothing could be so erroneous.
She said she never felt a lack of love for me
or with me.
I have never bored her.
How honored, how grateful,
how astounded I am that I interest her.
I kiss her neck warmly –
wanting her.

Each moment –
I pined for her;
I longed for her –
I desired her.
Some legacies can't last.
Some duets aren't sustainable.
But we have staying power.
It is strong as the galaxy's tightest muscle.
We have resilience.
Soft as a butterfly kiss.
I'd expected her to stop loving me –
of course I did.
Deep down, within the soul of me,
I knew better.
We won't disappear from one another's lives.
That isn't even a remote possibility.
In the world's immense vastness –
we belong.
In the immeasurable universe -
we monopolize one another's dreams.
I was a sidekick –
but I'd impacted her.
Now I am the best investment she ever made.
No one could ever love her more.
My only true enterprise was my desire for her
and for her happiness.
We shall live together for all times
in the Realm of Belonging.

Nomadic Habitat

What a classic nomadic habitat we built.
We'd dashed across the epic novel of our life.
We read notes
coming from across half a continent.
Those words materialized in flares.
Each moment I want the romance of her.
We no longer live on the edge of oblivion.
Codified words were often indelible.
Expressions zip along
the cyber path in milliseconds.
Ethereal unions
between scribblers sometimes eroded.
Our messages are footnoted.
We sip glasses of fine wine.
Clinking goblets,
we toast the complexity.
Her beautiful eyes transcribed
each well-formed moment of allure.
Our laughter sputters and our smiles lurch.
I taste the lips of unabbreviated desire.
We share the caresses
of arms enfolding our entirety.
Our embrace has become our home.
Delving inside the preciousness of us,
I notice our habitat
is always going to be nomadic.
We wouldn't want it any other way.

Torchlight Extravaganza

Our seasons are loaded up with entertainment.
We line up with the enchantment
of our nights together.
We arrive at the center of a torchlight extravaganza.
Time sings out our names – and we attend.
It is a narrow road when happiness accompanies us.
Amusement tosses laughter at us.
We search each grasp of contentment.
We know its location by heart.
Silence is an option that allows festivity.
Daily blessings pelt us with shelter.
Beneath the sanctuary of pleasure, we stabilize.

I am mirth's recruit.
Center stage – we share the spotlight.
We have one another's candid appreciation.
We eavesdrop on one another's passion.
The night air is perfumed
with a scented floral mist.
Your mouth tastes of cinnamon.
Your enormous blinking eyes issue a direct invitation.
Darkness changes your sapphire eyes to jade lakes.
Your exquisite body moves nearer mine –
requesting my presence and enticing me.
Spicy romance is in your teasing smile.
Your limber body is a tie-breaker.
Jubilation - of course – you are accomplished.
We bring one another exultation.
Fun is our sunshine and our pastime.
Life is our torchlight and our extravaganza.

Shelter and Solace

Lift off – floating solo, we are.
Existence can never be a completely shared act.
We are born, we breathe, and our hearts throbs.
We deliberate our quest to live.
We seek our place of tranquility and comfort.
Most of us find love's shelter and solace.
A tuft of floral elegance brings us together.
Being cherished gives us the plaudits
we need to survive.
If unloved – life is diminished.
Without affection – what is left?
Within our planetary cadence is our pulsing.
We allow one another to provide a place.
We reside within our sequence.
There is such kindness
in the correct honor of love.
I am prized and she is adored.
We borrow and lend compassion, attention,
and one another.
Her lips reach my soul; her kiss holds my heart.
As a butterfly lights up the earth
with gliding color,
our eyes gleam for one another.
And we gather together
throughout life's generosity.
She is my shelter and she is my solace.
And I am hers.

Artistic Endeavor

Our obsession is called creativity.
Grueling, frightening, and imposing –
the artistic endeavor overrides all else.
Each hectic word, each note,
each swipe of the brush is compelling.
It is necessity for the artist's reason.

Working without a Muse
is like working without a net.
My own Muse has taken me on meteoric travels.
Women are my grand legacy.
Our inheritance was born of heart-words.
Temptresses invite me to view a creative spirit.

My woman claims
I'm involved in a ménage a trios.
Perhaps she's right –
my Muse is seated to one side.
My Lady is on the other.
Oh, my!
Have I admitted that?
I am because of my Muse.
I am for and forever my woman's keepsake.
They are both prophesies
of my artistic endeavors.

Couples

We are one another's team.
We agreed that the mechanics
of being a couple include regulations.
If romance is in the center –
only constellations remain.
The polarity insists on tenderness, sensitivity,
and consideration.
We enrich one another.
Compelling answers
come with humility's questions.
Coupling is an addition – not a subtraction.
We evolved beside one another.
We come to believe in safeguards.
We enroll in our cottage of sweet moments.
We agree to sacrifice to the point of exhaustion.
Allegations and tirades must move aside.
Then cohabitation can sizzle.
Our signatures mingle.
We won't outgrow our adored spouse –
for we take our trips together every moment.
Love enriches us through the years.
We generate the cherished sharing.
Our equilibrium never diminishes.
Our rhetoric navigates away from blemishes.
We won't detach because we are irreplaceable.
Clues are information announcing
that we still care.
We are still altruistic companions.
We know how to whisper forgiveness –
and how to hear it.
There's no need to focus on a verdict.
Our win is together.

Aphrodisiac

We are one another's aphrodisiac.
Love is soft flower petals
touching us both at one time.
We concoct a luscious potion.
When it comes to blueprints –
I am an impoverished poet.
Prose is also my melody.
Even colloquialism inserts itself.
Words – sweet and tender are whispered.
Smiling begins our romance.
Floating through your lips,
across your tongue,
is a lingering invitation.
Our dance melds us warmly together.
Cuddling is the embrace of Goddesses.
You are my gourmet delight.
Our chemistry is an invincible incentive.
I gobble up the luxury of you.
I gulp down the aphrodisiac of you.

Savory Heartbeat

We whispered *Lover* into every memory.
Our seasons hurry us – leisure often eludes us.
Each moment is precious when we embrace.
Arms gather around one another's waists.
I never want to let go.
Aware there is always a great stopwatch in the sky,
we realize we can defy it – but not outrun it.
So we commit each blink of time to memory.
Hours quicken in tempo – each of them ours.
Our lullaby becomes a waltz – and a sweet ballad.
We fold together through our nights.
We awaken with the clutch of dawn.
We digest the smile of love's savory gloss.
Through it all, we endure – we continue.
Our creed is perpetual – is eternal.
There is total recall of our synchronizing glimpse.
Yours is the most savory heartbeat in the world.

Cantilevered Over Desire

Recruited romance changed me.
I was a willing participant.
I hungered for the victory of you.
Perhaps valor is pathos without acrimony.
You are the diva that scores highest.
I'm daunted by your loveliness.
Your allure is like no other.
I have officially been captured
by a magnetizing, wily woman.
You.
You and your kisses!
What poetical evocation passed by my lips?
We became simultaneous.
You took away the scratches on my heart.
I was conscripted into love.
Walking the trails, the paths –
we practiced searching for kindness.
Reclining in the meadows –
we touched the flesh of loyalty and lust.
We stood on a mountain ledge.
It was cantilevered over desire.

Fetching Delight

Chance had been our meeting of choice.
I sat at the bar beside a pugnacious dyke.
Rebellion was carved on her face.
Her very stern features had been chiseled.
She'd never opened a cookbook –
but she knew women inside and out.
And they liked her,
or they admired her.
Men were ignored by her.
And when they intruded –
it was their misfortune.
She'd probably been a sparring partner –
she learned to smash apart the bullies.

Billie – she was named Billie.
No one crossed her.
She gave an imitation of lethargy.
But when she moved,
she was a million pound wrecking ball.
With women,
her stoicism germinated bliss.
Nobody condemned her chutzpah.
Everyone condoned her colorful vocabulary.
Her devotees would exterminate the gods
on her behalf.
Her enemies were thwacked to defeat,
but not without her admonition.
Billie didn't like distraction.
As we chatted,
I shut up when her favorite song played.
I never interrupted.
Keeping my conviviality up front,
I always agreed.

Hey Kid, she called to me,
you got a date tonight?

No, I answered –
perhaps a little too complacently.
Deadpan, she looked away.
And you ain't getting' any chick
if you act so fuckin' unconscious.
My life trickled before me –
I feared a collision.
It's my shyness,
I confessed with a stutter -
as if absentia was my only alternative.
You need to be flamboyant – dynamic,
and you ain't even close.
I objected, *No one seems very friendly.*
She grinned and challenged,
You just don't know how the hell to fetch delight.

A decade later, I entered the bar and saw Billie.
She asked, *Where you been, Kid?'*
I first introduced her to my lady.
I've been settled down, I then reported.
Humph, she grumbled,
How'd you ever get a woman?
I wouldn't mention
that I'd taken her recommendation.
I'd tried fetching delight.
But the glint in her eyes told me
she suspected as much.

Poetic Blueprints

Poets aren't easily managed.
Blueprints might help with their construction –
and with behavior.
Misconduct isn't amusing, for starters.
Five-syllable words
were clustered into a verbal fist.
Before spitting them out,
I swallowed them.
It wouldn't have worked for party chatter.
Poets can be vanquished for 'word' aristocracy.
Flocking as a pack
can be viewed as marching-hostility.
Being prematurely induced into romance –
not a good idea.
Don't trip and fall over erogenous zones.
Fragile balance is much more normal.
Don't chase perpetual heat – the burn unit is full.
Hiding in heaven's attic –
not interesting.
Don't be gregarious
to the point of tumbling down.
Stoic inversion never makes a person authentic.
No one is made of euphemisms.
Poets normally dress up in androgyny.
Arousing desire doesn't demand narcissism.
Never mention that a trip has been taken
into hell's bunker.
Don't brag about a lascivious background.
Just say the devil snarls.
Acting as if eavesdropping
makes women think an echo is following.
Eroticism may take a little espionage –
but put away all notebooks when delving.
Remember how isolation is also chaotic –
so go ahead and ask her for a date.
Loving her might create
an amazingly wonderful poem.

Captivating and Youthful Amaretto

In our youth,
Amaretto was captivating –
the women were sweet –
our longing was sensual.
Our password was *fun*.
Poised for revolution,
we expected to rearrange society.
We were weekend warriors
pilgrimaging for our pride.
We were flower children –
replete with playbills of equality.
We loved the underdog –
we were the underdog.
We were quirky by choice.
We disapproved of Fascist tendencies.
And we were never ambivalent toward power.
We were animated by our budding youth –
and were exalted by our promise.
We were connoisseurs
of great worldly feasts.
Gourmet meals were served
at our Festival of Spring.
Our rites – our rights?
We found out about them
the day before someone told us the truth.
We realized then that treachery was incognito.
We became aware of our vulnerabilities.
The haters had misspelled the words
scandalous lesbian perverts.
What the hell is a scand-las lez-b-ain pre-vert?
I knew which one I was.
I didn't care then – I care even less now.
Our summer trepidation excluded most bullies.
They were sneaky and hidden.
They even infiltrated our rites.
Youth's synopsis can be painful.

By the time winter garb is worn –
a world has mellowed.
Or we have.
As season's slipper-slide down time's ride –
we articulate those celebratory moments.
Mostly forgotten are the slurs and the hatred.
Proverbs explain the universe in a one-line whisper.
Remember the amaretto-sweet women.

A Singular Poet

I
Laconically, we struggle to dust our spirits.
We pant after our best vision.
Nightmares are owned by all writers.
Sometimes annihilating monsters
isn't possible.
As we are reaching for promise and victory -
loneliness might appear.
Masochism loads dreams
and disappears in whispers.
Shadows are tarnished, and menacing.
Reality defeats danger.
Vulnerability extinguishes pride.
Even exotic eyes appear null and void.
Lurching after songs about rain – we drift.
We rendezvous with visitors.
The gates of yesterday fan open.
We find safety there –
because smiles rescue one another.

II
When our keyboard shuts down –
the alphabet snags.
Prose is sung, and dialogue is confirmed.
Yet it is too lifeless to produce pearled gray fog.
Rushing thought presses onto pages.
Meandering emotion is unalterable –
and doesn't want to be disturbed.
We try to translate woe from glow.
Anger needs to be laundered.
We share our satchel of intrigue.
Guilt is a poison-dipped arrow.
A quill pen bounces away
from ink-stained fingers.
The final line is a sensory plot.

III
Unabridged versions can reach us.
But we must create the version together.
Our past abridgement creeps away from us.
We establish an amatory grasp.
Passion is converted
by hot energy into aesthetic words.
Our souls are drenched in unison.
Cloudbursts reach their crescendo,
and we are one another's pinnacle.
Emanating through us is concern.
Exchanging spirits is complex.
Our reflective souls cling
to the skin that covers us.
We wear our drenched flesh proudly.
With the fragility of a blink –
we are offered to one another.
We've each been alone – very alone.
We sing another verse.
Poetry is difficult to rearrange.
Solo – it is – alone I am.
For only I can touch the nudity of my heart.

A Woman Named Unremarkable

I've never met a woman named unremarkable.
I doubt if one ever existed.
Each woman *is* remarkable.
In her own way,
each feminine heart is filled with sunshine.
Naturally,
there are women that ignore their own magic.
They fail to appreciate the very wonder
of themselves.
I'm proud to be a woman, and to love women.
We aren't now, nor have we ever been,
the weaker sex.
We aren't the second sex, the lesser sex,
and we aren't inferior.
In some tribes we may be underestimated,
and underrated.
Some societies and many beliefs would lecture
that we're subordinates.
They wish to stress our inadequacies.
Women are never unremarkable,
and never inadequate.
The female sex comprises of paramours,
lovers, mistresses, sweethearts, and wives.
We are mothers, sisters,
daughters, and friends.
Our strength can only be realized from knowing
how truly valued we are.
Each woman is a marvel,
a survivor, and a champion.
We are miraculous, tender, and we are splendid.
Perhaps it is only when we forget our deity
that we present ourselves otherwise.
Each of us needs to give, and be given,
our approval, our recognition,
and our appreciation for and to other women.
We must prop one another up.

We've got to recognize how truly remarkable we are.
I do not know any unremarkable women.
When I look into the faces of all women –
I see sunshine and stars.

Unlocked Woman

Beginning, we are sealed tightly.
Uninterrupted, we are stored away.
Eroticism is discarded – until we're ready.
Souls aren't empty – they just aren't shown.
We don't unravel inside one another.
We ignite and orbit the heat of one another.
When we partake in love – our limbs go limp.
Our dreams are exposed.
Our inhibitions are suspended.
The contours of us glide against one another.
We try to fit into our own souls.
Passion pelts us.
We dismantle our apprehension.
The froth of love is scrolled
as we exchange emotion.
Although we share – and exchange –
we never become one another.
Our draping shawls loop together by softness.
Our smudged mistrust unstitches if we allow it.
Past hurts puncture unless we nestle near.
Ascending words are traded.
Fragmented memories are durable.
We accomplished and sustained the hope of us.
For we unlock at the same moment
with the woman we love.

Longing and Belonging

Our name was Longing.
Our romance was Belonging.
Some affection has no name.
Some affairs are in lower case.
Our love is in bold capital letters.
We've scripted one another
with all that we are.
There is no other option – only passion.
Our spirits have been super-glued to one another.
Our own backyard is the world.
The revival of us has been hosted by angels.
Time's pulse slows with rushed moments –
in an attempt to keep up
with our rhythmic bodies.
I long for you while running this race
across the greatness of eternity.
I wish to give tribute to you.
I scream across a wide corridor
of commitment.
I give your softly sculpted cheek
a tender caress.
I press your honey-bronze hair
between my fingers.
Its silkiness thrills my senses.
Your wondrous blue eyes
harness my affection.
Your mellow lips kiss my smile.
We had longed for matching hearts.
Now that they belong to us,
we belong.
It is our realm.

Kieran York

Author Kieran York

Kieran York

About the Author

Kieran York is the author of lesbian fiction and poetry. She authored the lesbian mystery series featuring Royce Madison in the mid-1990s. _Timber City Masks_ and _Crystal Mountain Veils_ were reissued in 2014-2015 by Scarlet Clover Publishers LLC. In the late 1980s, York wrote a collection of lesbian short stories entitled _Sugar With Spice._

In 2012, her book of fiction, _Appointment with a Smile,_ was published and was a 2013 Lambda Literary Society Award Finalist in the Romance category. Her next novel, _Careful Flowers,_ was released in 2013. Both books were published by Blue Feather Books, and second editions republished by Scarlet Clover Publishers.

In 2014, Scarlet Clover Publishers LLC, released _Earthen Trinkets_ and _Night Without Time._ In 2015, _Loitering on the Frontier_ and _Touring Kelly's Poem_ were published.

York was also a contributor in _Sappho's Corner Poetry Series – Wet Violets, Volume 2; Roses Read, Volume 3; Delectable Daisies, Volume 4; and Fallen Petals, Volume 5._

In 2014, her volume of poetry, _Blushing Aspen,_ was published as the Sappho's Corner Solo Poet book of poetry.

Previously, during the seventies, and eighties, Kieran worked as a reporter and reviewer for both newspaper and magazine and was a magazine publisher for three years. She also wrote and performed songs with a women's band.

She has been guest lecturer and panel member at various events, including Rocky Mountain Book Exhibition, Colorado Musicians Series, Sisters in Crime Mystery

Writers, and Mystery Writers of America, Inc. She is a member of Lambda Literary Society and Golden Crown Literary Society.

She has written for *Journal of Mystery Readers International*. In addition, she has given numerous campus and coffeehouse readings, as well as taught poetry and creative writing workshops.

York graduated from a Kansas university and attended Mexico's University of the Americas her junior year. She has done - not completed, graduate work at the University of Colorado.

Kieran lives in the Rocky Mountain foothills of Colorado with her schnauzer, Clover. She enjoys gardening, music, literature, and art. She considers her valuables to include Clover and other family and friends, her library, her antique typewriter collection, and her guitar.

Additional information is available on her website. She has a blog – Embellish Your smile at http://kieranyork.com.

FORTHCOMING IN 2015...

Shinney Forest Cloaks

In the third Royce Madison mystery, Sheriff Royce Madison and her deputies are searching for a missing woman. The newcomer to Timber County disappears without a trace.

Royce not only has her hands full with this crime, her personal life seems to be falling apart. She is no facing her midlife crisis. Things aren't the same, and perhaps never again can be the way they once were. She longs for tranquility in the Colorado mountain town. And in her own life.

Within Our Celebration

Short fiction book will be released in late summer. Serious, quirky, in love and in life - the people you know and are. Short stories will range from comedy to drama. Life in Lesbos, frontier women – lesbians in various aspects of modern life – all age groups, social groups – women who love women. They are our stories about riding this globe within our celebration!

OTHER PUBLISHED TITLES BY KIERAN YORK

Fiction:

Sugar With Spice
Publisher: Banned Books (November 1989)

Timber City Masks
Publisher: Third Side Press, 1st Edition (May 1993)
Publisher: Scarlet Clover Publishers, 2nd Edition, (November 2014)

Crystal Mountain Veils
Publisher: Third Side Press, 1st Edition (April 1995)
Publisher: Scarlet Clover Publishers, 2nd Edition, (January 2015)

Appointment with a Smile
Publisher: Blue Feather Books, 1st Edition (March 2012)
Publisher: Scarlet Clover Publishers, 2nd Edition (January 2015)

Careful Flowers
Publisher: Blue Feather Books, 1st Edition (October 2013)
Publisher: Scarlet Clover Publishers, 2nd Edition (January 2015)

Earthen Trinkets
Publisher: Scarlet Clover Publishers, (September 2014)

Night Without Time
Publisher: Scarlet Clover Publishers, (November 2014)

Touring Kelly's Poem
Publisher: Scarlet Clover Publishers, (February, 2015)

Loitering on the Frontier
Publisher: Scarlet Clover Publishers, (March, 2015)

Poetry:

Blushing Aspen
Publisher: UltraVioletLove Publishing, (May 2014)